The media's watching Va
Here's a sampling of our (

CW01021490

"[Vault tells] prospective joiners what they really want to know about the culture, the interview process, the salaries and the job prospects."
- *The Financial Times*

"Thanks to Vault, the truth about work is just a tap of your keyboard away."
- *The Telegraph*

"The best place on the Web to prepare for a job search."
– *Fortune*

"For those hoping to climb the ladder of success, [Vault's] insights are priceless."
– *Money* magazine

"A killer app."
– *The New York Times*

"To get the unvarnished scoop, check out Vault."
– *Smart Money* magazine

"Vault has a wealth of information about major employers and job-searching strategies as well as comments from workers about their experiences at specific companies."
– *The Washington Post*

VAULT
> the most trusted name in career information™

VAULT CAREER GUIDE TO

INVESTMENT
BANKING

EUROPEAN EDITION

Tom Lott, Richard Roberts
and the staff of vault

For information about permission to reproduce selections from this book, contact Vault Inc., 150 West 22nd St, New York, New York 10011, (212) 366-4212.

Library of Congress CIP Data is available.

ISBN 13: 978-1-58131-514-1

ISBN 10: 1-58131-514-7

Printed in the United Kingdom

ACKNOWLEDGMENTS

We are extremely grateful to Vault's entire staff for all their help in the editorial, production and marketing processes. Vault also would like to acknowledge the support of our investors, clients, employees, family, and friends. Thank you!

JPMORGAN
WHO, WHAT AND WHY?

From the start, JPMorgan's goal has been to do first-class business in a first-class way. Over one century on, this hasn't changed. JPMorgan remains an industry innovator, forcing the pace of change in global finance and executing first-class business in a first-class way for clients across the globe.

Investment banking is a fast-moving world where talented people can achieve great things. If you're looking for responsibility and the chance to make an impact at an early stage in your career, then JPMorgan is the place for you. The application of new technology, fresh ideas, changing markets and a pipeline of high-quality work all unite to make JPMorgan an exhilarating place to work.

Business Profile

JPMorgan is the investment banking division of JPMorgan Chase & Co., an international financial services firm with more than $1.6 trillion in assets. JPMorgan offers its clients a differentiated platform with the most complete and innovative solutions to meet their evolving financial needs. The investment bank consistently ranks at the top of banking league tables and wins industry awards from major financial publications across the globe. Parent company, JPMorgan Chase, which is a component of the Dow Jones Industrial Average, also boasts powerful asset management, commercial banking, private banking, securities and treasury operations. JPMorgan's clients include corporations, institutional investors, hedge funds, governments and affluent individuals from more than 100 countries.

The JPMorgan brand encompasses six key business areas:

Investment Banking is the division that helps companies decide on marketplace strategy; advises clients on mergers and acquisitions; and provides access to the debt and equity markets. There are four key areas: Country Mergers & Acquisitions, Pan-European Sector Teams, Country Capital Markets and Securitised Products. In 2005, JPMorgan formed a joint venture with Cazenove, one of the U.K.'s top corporate brokers. Today, JPMorgan Cazenove is a major part of JPMorgan's U.K. investment banking operations.

Sales, Trading & Research is the collective name given to JPMorgan's Foreign Exchange, Commodities, Equities, Credit, Rates and Emerging Markets businesses. Traders execute and price transactions worth billions, while Sales provide the vital link between clients, traders and the research teams. Researchers provide market insights and recommend market strategies and Marketers fill the gap between those who create products and those who sell them.

Asset Management refers to the teams who manage investments for a broad spectrum of institutional and retail investors, including pension funds, governments, insurance companies and private individuals. With an overall AUM (assets under management) of US$1.2 trillion to invest on behalf of a diversified group of global clients, JPMorgan's Asset Management business isn't governed by short-term shifts in the markets. The challenge is to deliver the best possible return through the intelligent use of investment vehicles ranging from currency and equities to fixed income and real estate.

Risk understand and manage risk effectively to minimize unexpected results and generate revenues through lending, trading and capital markets activity. Risk Managers enjoy high profile roles that have a visible influence on the performance of the bank across the entire product range. Risk is broken down into five areas: Credit Risk, Market Risk, Operational Risk, Legal Risk and Reputation Risk.

Operations, Finance & Business Management provide the functions and processes that underpin all sales, trading, cash management and investment banking activities.

Operations look after the full end-to-end management of a transaction from the time that it is booked.

Finance is accountable for delivering key financial data for individual business areas and the overall results of the firm.

Business Management supports JPMorgan's strategic development as well as driving change within the organization. Teams work in partnership with colleagues from Technology and Corporate Infrastructure and are continually striving to increase revenues, improve efficiency and reduce risk.

Technology drives business innovation ensuring the company's competitive edge and making new things possible for clients. This area is growing in influence every year as JPMorgan invests billions of dollars in the infrastructure and applications that keep the firm at the forefront of the industry.

Recent Transactions and Awards

JPMorgan offers clients an unrivaled breadth and depth of capabilities and provides innovative ideas and flawless execution to clients across the globe. In 2007, JPMorgan acted as exclusive financial advisor to Vivendi/SFR on a transaction worth $12.3 billion; advised Ingersoll-Rand on its $10.1 billion acquisition of Trane Inc; acted as joint global coordinator and joint book runner on Sony Financial's IPO (JPY 320 billion); and was the sole bookrunner on the $1 billion Sukuk convertible bond issue for Dana Gas. In 2008, JPMorgan advised Reuters on the Reuters/Thomson deal worth some $18 billion.

JPMorgan has also won a number of prestigious industry awards:

- *Institutional Investor* – Best Overall Investment Bank

- *Risk Magazine* – Best Derivatives House over the past 20 years / Best Derivatives House of the Year for 2008 / Best Credit Derivatives House – Pioneer & Modern Great / Energy Derivatives House of the Year

- *The Banker* – Investment Bank of the Year: Americas / Bond Trading House of the Year / Financial Institutions Group Capital Raising House of the Year / Loans House of the Year

- *IFR* – Credit Derivatives House of the Year / Structured Equity House – Europe & US

- *Financial News* – Equity Linked Bank of the Year / UK M&A House of the Year

- *The Times* list of the UK's Top 50 companies Where Women Want to Work (second year running)

The Hot Six

Six is the magic number.

When JPMorgan asked their people 'why work at JPMorgan?' they couldn't think of a single reason - they thought of six. These are the Hot Six, the top six reasons to choose JPMorgan, as chosen by JPMorgan people across all levels, business groups and geographies:

1. Scale, scope and prestige.

With 34,000 of the world's finest minds across the Investment Bank and Asset Management, in over 50 countries, you could be doing business just about anywhere. Precisely what you'll be doing will depend on your own ambitions, professionally and personally. JPMorgan have been defining the world of finance for over 100 years, with a trillion-dollar enterprise and a full-service platform. **This is where you'll benefit from JPMorgan's global success.**

2. Reputation as a business innovator.

Innovation has driven JPMorgan from the earliest days, and continues to drive the business now. JPMorgan is the bank that built corporate America, rescued the New York Stock Exchange, created the world's first billion-dollar corporation, invented the concept of relationship banking and pioneered in derivatives.

Today, the firm combines unprecedented global leverage in the markets with an entrepreneurial zeal that allows employees to explore every facet of the Investment Banking industry. **JPMorgan is where you'll think in new ways.**

3. The quality of training and development.

Training doesn't automatically cease as soon as you finish being a 'graduate.' Your trainers will include professors from the world's best business schools, JPMorgan leaders and over 500 senior JPMorgan bankers. The theoretical and the practical are combined at JPMorgan like nowhere else.

The training and development programs on offer are the very best in the sector, with Vault ranking JPMorgan the Best Training Program out of all Investment and Commercial Banks in 2007. **At JPMorgan you'll never stop learning.**

4. The chance to make a personal impact.

JPMorgan encourages and celebrates high performance. It's the firm's belief that the individual can only flourish as part of the team, for the benefit of all involved. On the job, your responsibilities and contributions will be substantial and development and promotion are often rapidly gained. **JPMorgan is where you can make a name for yourself.**

5. The exceptional quality of work.

You'll be given opportunities every day – and right from the very start. You'll enjoy exposure to a quick-flowing pipeline of varied and high-quality work. You can work on the world's top deals, manage money for the most sophisticated investors, make the most complex trades or launch the most cutting-edge products in global finance. The challenges you face will test you professionally and drive you to develop personally. **You will master complex challenges at JPMorgan.**

6. The spirit of cooperation and teamwork.
JPMorgan's many successes would not have been possible were it not for the open, intellectually productive culture which exists in the firm. JPMorgan is a global network of the finest minds. The bank expects people to bounce ideas off one another, to support one another and to respect one another. **JPMorgan is where you'll inspire, support, and connect.**

Preparing Leaders

JPMorgan is excellent at helping high-potential individuals turn into high-performers. The training programs combine on-the-job learning with classroom instruction that is on a par with the world's finest business schools. As a result, junior Analysts emerge not only with a thorough grounding in their own business area, but also with a broad understanding of the wider commercial picture and a range of transferable skills from project management to team leadership.

Can You Do This?

JPMorgan currently recruits into Investment Banking, Sales, Trading & Research, Risk, Asset Management, Operations, Finance & Business Management and Technology. Candidates have to meet stringent requirements and the firm expects exceptional academic qualifications. Individuals should have a strong interest in the business, but curiosity, drive, initiative, communication skills and intelligence are also vital.

JPMorgan recruits from all disciplines and the firm looks to draw from the broadest, smartest talent pool in the world. Academic credentials are important, but so too are achievements outside of the classroom. Applicants must have an expected minimum degree of a 2:1 or European equivalent and fluency in English is a pre-requisite.

There are many ways in which you can get to know JPMorgan better. Applying for a place on one of JPMorgan's many initiatives is one of them. From first year programs in the Spring and Autumn aimed at demystifying Investment Banking, to online simulated trading games and philanthropic competitions, it doesn't matter what stage of your education you're at, there will be something to suit you.

Vault Survey Results

Below are some quotations from Vault's own Investment Banking industry survey, research findings and employee feedback.

Preserving its legacy

JPMorgan's culture is described as "extremely international and very relaxed" where "people are not expected to fit a mould". Overall, one associate says, "[The culture] makes for an open, productive work environment" although respondents agree that there's a "cut to the chase," "competitive" feeling to the firm. That said, people also "know how to be relaxed and civility is the rule of the day at a firm where "managers have always maintained an open-door policy."

Climbing the curve

"Face time is not required" at JPMorgan, but as one associate puts it, "the learning curve is very steep and that motivates people to put the extra time in." Another concurs, "No one is looking over your shoulder to see when you get in or when you leave but the top performers are usually the hardest workers."

The personal touch

JPMorgan "is known for an extraordinarily rigorous hiring process," sources say. However, as one managing director explained, that is because "the firm is in the fortunate position of being able to select from the brightest and most diverse group of applicants in the business."

So what do those who make it in banking have in common? "The distinguishing factor is not only having the qualifications to work here, but knowing why you want to work here," a current employee says. At JPMorgan, recruiters ultimately look at candidates for the long run: "We're hiring future leaders of our respective business, not simply candidates for an entry-level position," one insider reveals.

JPMorgan

JPMorgan ⬡

OVER TO YOU.

200 years of industry-defining success. A tradition of innovation. A team spirit that supports the individual. And a future that's more exciting than anything that's gone before.

So who do we trust to carry our name forward? We don't know yet, but we'd like to find out. Visit our website for more details on the challenges and rewards you'll enjoy throughout your career. You're our next generation. **This is where you need to be.**

jpmorgan.com/careers

Table of Contents

Visit **Vault Europe's Finance Career Channel** at **www.Vault.com/Europe** for insider firm profiles, employee surveys of banking profesionals in Europe, job listings, expert finance career advice, insider salary information and more.

VAULT   CAREER LIBRARY   xv

JPMorgan

JUST HOW GOOD CAN YOU BE?

"We have an outstanding strategic position, a great brand, strong character, fantastic employees and a remarkable future. I am privileged to lead this company. I don't know yet how good we can be." Jamie Dimon, Chairman and CEO, JPMorgan.

This is where you need to be.

jpmorgan.com/careers

THE
INDUSTRY

What is Investment Banking?

CHAPTER 1

What is investment banking? Is it investing? Is it banking? Really, it is neither. Investment banking, or I-banking, as it is often called, is the term used to describe the business of raising capital for companies and advising them on financing and merger alternatives. Capital essentially means money. Companies need cash in order to grow and expand their businesses; investment banks sell securities to public investors in order to raise this cash. These securities can come in the form of stocks or bonds, which we will discuss in depth later.

The Players

The biggest investment banks include Morgan Stanley, Credit Suisse, Citigroup, JPMorgan, Deutsche Bank and UBS, among others. Of course, the complete list of I-banks is more extensive, but the firms listed above compete for the biggest deals worldwide.

In the European market there is also a number of major regional players, including Rothschild, ABN Amro, Lazard, BNP Paribas, Mediobanca, Societe Generale, Dresdner Kleinwort Wasserstein, HSBC Holdings and Barclays Capital.

Many an I-banking interviewee asks, "Which firm is the best?" The answer, like many things in life, is unclear. There are many ways to measure the quality of investment banks. You might examine a bank's expertise in a certain segment of investment banking. For example, Citigroup was tops globally in 2005 in total debt and equity underwriting volume, but trailed Goldman Sachs in mergers and acquisitions ("M&A") advisory. Goldman Sachs has a stellar reputation in equity underwriting and M&A advisory but is not as strong in debt issuance. Those who watch the industry pay attention to "league tables," which are rankings of investment banks in several categories (e.g., equity underwriting or M&A advisory). The most commonly referred to league tables are published quarterly by Thomson Financial, a research firm based in Newark, N.J. Thomson collects data on deals done in a given time period and determines which firm has done the most deals in a given sector over that time period. Essentially, the league tables are rankings of firm by quantity of deals in a given area.

Vault also provides prestige rankings of the Top 50 banking firms, based on surveys of finance professionals. These rankings are available on our web site, www.vault.com.

Visit **Vault Europe's Finance Career Channel** at **www.Vault.com/Europe** for insider firm profiles, employee surveys of banking profesionals in Europe, job listings, expert finance career advice, insider salary information and more.

VAULT CAREER LIBRARY 3

Of course, industry rankings and prestige ratings don't tell a firm's whole story. Since the pay scale in the industry tends to be comparable among different firms, potential investment bankers would be wise to pay attention to the quality of life at the firms they're considering for employment. This includes culture, social life and hours. You can glean this information from your job interviews as well as reports on the firms available from Vault.

The Game

Generally, the breakdown of an investment bank includes the following areas:

Corporate Finance (equity)
Corporate Finance (debt)
Mergers & Acquisitions (M&A)
Equity Sales
Fixed Income Sales
Syndicate (equity)
Syndicate (debt)
Equity Trading
Fixed Income Trading
Equity Research
Fixed Income Research

The functions of all of these areas will be discussed in much more detail later in the book. In this overview section, we will cover the nuts and bolts of the business, providing an overview of the stock and bond markets, and how an I-bank operates within them.

Corporate finance

The bread and butter of a traditional investment bank, corporate finance generally performs two different functions: 1) Mergers and acquisitions advisory and 2) Underwriting. On the mergers and acquisitions (M&A) advising side of corporate finance, bankers assist in negotiating and structuring a merger between two companies. If, for example, a company wants to buy another firm, then an investment bank will help finalize the purchase price, structure the deal, and generally ensure a smooth transaction. The underwriting function within corporate finance involves shepherding the process of raising capital for a company. In the investment banking world, capital can be raised by selling either stocks or bonds (as well as some more exotic securities) to investors.

Sales

Sales is another core component of any investment bank. Salespeople take the form of: 1) the classic retail broker, 2) the institutional salesperson, or 3) the private client service representative. Retail brokers develop relationships with individual investors and sell

Visit **Vault Europe's Finance Career Channel** at **www.Vault.com/Europe** for insider firm profiles, employee surveys of banking profesionals in Europe, job listings, expert finance career advice, insider salary information and more.

VAULT CAREER LIBRARY

5

stocks and stock advice to the average Joe. Institutional salespeople develop business relationships with large institutional investors. Institutional investors are those who manage large groups of assets, for example pension funds, mutual funds, or large corporations. Private Client Service (PCS) representatives lie somewhere between retail brokers and institutional salespeople, providing brokerage and money management services for extremely wealthy individuals. Salespeople make money through commissions on trades made through their firms or, increasingly, as a percentage of their clients' assets with the firm.

Trading

Traders also provide a vital role for the investment bank. In general, traders facilitate the buying and selling of stocks, bonds, and other securities such as currencies and futures, either by carrying an inventory of securities for sale or by executing a given trade for a client.

A trader plays two distinct roles for an investment bank:

(1) Providing liquidity: Traders provide liquidity to the firm's clients (that is, providing clients with the ability to buy or sell a security on demand). Traders do this by standing ready to immediately buy the client's securities (or sell securities to the client) if the client needs to place a trade quickly. This is also called making a market, or acting as a market maker. Traders performing this function make money for the firm by selling securities at a slightly higher price than they pay for them. This price differential is known as the bid-ask spread. (The bid price at any given time is the price at which customers can sell a security, which is usually slightly lower than the ask price, which is the price at which customers can buy the same security.)

(2) Proprietary trading: In addition to providing liquidity and executing traders for the firm's customers, traders also may take their own trading positions on behalf of the firm, using the firm's capital hoping to benefit from the rise or fall in the price of securities. This is called proprietary trading. Typically, the marketing-making function and the proprietary trading function is performed by the same trader for any given security.

In recent years, executives who cut their teeth on the trading floor have risen to the top of many leading investment banks. Their elevation reflects the growing importance of trading to investment bank profits.

Research

Research analysts follow stocks and bonds and make recommendations on whether to buy, sell, or hold those securities. They also forecast companies' future earnings. Stock analysts (known as equity analysts) typically focus on one industry and will cover up to 20 companies' stocks at any given time. Some research analysts work on the fixed income side and will cover a particular segment, such as a particular industry's high yield bonds. Salespeople within the I-bank utilize research published by analysts to convince their clients to buy or sell securities through their firm. Corporate finance bankers rely on research analysts to be experts in the industry in which they are working. Reputable research analysts can generate substantial corporate finance business for their firm as well as substantial trading activity, and thus are an integral part of any investment bank.

Syndicate

The hub of the investment banking wheel, the syndicate group provides a vital link between salespeople and corporate finance. Syndicate exists to facilitate the placing of securities in a public offering, a knock-down drag-out affair between and among buyers of offerings and the investment banks managing the process. In a corporate or municipal debt deal, syndicate also determines the allocation of bonds.

Visit **Vault Europe's Finance Career Channel** at **www.Vault.com/Europe** for insider firm profiles, employee surveys of banking profesionals in Europe, job listings, expert finance career advice, insider salary information and more.

VAULT CAREER LIBRARY 7

Commercial Banking, Investment Banking and Asset Management

"Commercial bankers live off their deposits — investment bankers live off their wits," goes a traditional saying of the London financial markets that captures the key difference between the two types of banking activity.

Before analysing how an investment bank operates, let's explore the differences between commercial banking and investment banking — but also what they have in common.

Commercial Banking vs Investment Banking

The fundamental profit generating business activity of both commercial and investment banks is the provision of funds for borrowers. Commercial banks provide loans for the full spectrum of borrowers, from private individuals, through small businesses, to major "corporates" — large private companies, governments at the municipal, regional and national levels and other public entities. Commercial banks make loans to borrowers from the funds provided by the other side of their business — taking deposits from individuals and firms.

Investment banks mostly deal only with corporate level clients (though some have credit card arms). Investment banks do not take deposits — as a result some people dispute whether they should be called 'banks' at all. They raise funds for borrowers by acting as intermediaries for them in the financial markets. To do this effectively requires an appreciation of the funding needs of their clients and an intimate knowledge of the market — living off their wits.

Commercial banks

A **commercial bank** is licensed to take deposits — the funds that are paid into current (checking) and deposit (savings) accounts by its customers. Banks are highly regulated across Europe, though laws and regulatory arrangements vary from country to country. One reason is to protect the funds of depositors. Another is to safeguard the stability of the financial system, which is vitally important for the economy as a whole.

Visit **Vault Europe's Finance Career Channel** at www.Vault.com/Europe for insider firm profiles, employee surveys of banking profesionals in Europe, job listings, expert finance career advice, insider salary information and more.

VAULT CAREER LIBRARY

9

The typical commercial banking process is fairly straightforward. You deposit money into your bank, and the bank loans that money to consumers and companies in need of capital (cash). You borrow to buy a house, finance a car, or finance an addition to your home. Companies borrow to finance the growth of their company or meet immediate cash needs. Companies that borrow from commercial banks can range in size from the dry cleaner on the corner to a multinational conglomerate. The commercial bank generates a profit by paying depositors a lower interest rate than the bank charges on loans.

Private contracts

Importantly, loans from commercial banks are structured as private legally binding contracts between two parties — the bank and you (or the bank and a company). Banks work with their clients to individually determine the terms of the loans, including the time to maturity and the interest rate charged. Your individual credit history (or credit risk profile) determines the amount you can borrow and how much interest you are charged. Perhaps your company needs to borrow $200,000 over 15 years to finance the purchase of equipment, or maybe your firm needs $30,000 over five years to finance the purchase of a truck. Maybe for the first loan, you and the bank will agree that you pay an interest rate of 7.5 percent; perhaps for the truck loan, the interest rate will be 11 percent. The rates are determined through a negotiation between the bank and the company.

Let's take another minute to understand how a bank makes its money. On most loans, commercial banks in the U.S. earn interest anywhere from 5 to 14 percent. Ask yourself how much your bank pays you on your deposits — the money that it uses to make loans. You probably earn a paltry 1 percent on a checking account, if anything, and maybe 2 to 3 percent on a savings account. Commercial banks thus make money by taking advantage of the large spread between their cost of funds (1 percent, for example) and their return on funds loaned (ranging from 5 to 14 percent).

Investment banks

An investment bank operates differently. An investment bank does not have an inventory of cash deposits to lend as a commercial bank does. In essence, an investment bank acts as an intermediary, and matches sellers of stocks and bonds with buyers of stocks and bonds.

Note, however, that companies use investment banks toward the same end as they use commercial banks. If a company needs capital, it may get a loan from a bank, or it may ask an investment bank to sell equity or debt (stocks or bonds). Because commercial banks already have funds available from their depositors and an investment bank typically does not, an I-bank must spend considerable time finding investors in order to obtain capital for its client. (Note that as investment banks are increasingly seeking to become "one-stop" financing sources, many I-banks have set aside part of their own capital that they can use to loan to clients directly.)

Private Debt vs. Bonds — An Example

Let's look at an example to illustrate the difference between **private debt** and **bonds**. Suppose Acme Cleaning Company needs capital, and estimates its need to be $200 million. Acme could obtain a commercial bank loan from Bank of New York for the entire $200 million, and pay interest on that loan just like you would pay on a $2,000 personal finance loan from Bank of New York. Alternately, it could sell bonds publicly using an investment bank such as Merrill Lynch. The $200 million bond issue raised by Merrill would be broken into many smaller bonds and then sold to the public. (For example, the issue could be broken into 200,000 bonds, each worth $1,000.) Once sold, the company receives its $200 million (less Merrill's fees) and investors receive bonds worth a total of the same amount.

Over time, the investors in the bond offering receive coupon payments (the interest), and ultimately the principal (the original $1,000) at the end of the life of the loan, when Acme Corp buys back the bonds (retires the bonds). Thus, we see that in a bond offering, while the money is still loaned to Acme, it is actually loaned by numerous investors, rather than from a single bank.

Because the investment bank involved in the offering does not own the bonds but merely placed them with investors at the outset, it earns no interest — the bondholders earn this interest in the form of regular coupon payments. The investment bank makes money by charging the client (in this case, Acme) a small percentage of the transaction upon its completion. Investment banks call this upfront fee the "underwriting discount." In contrast, a commercial bank making a loan actually receives the interest and simultaneously owns the debt.

Later, we will cover the steps involved in underwriting a public bond deal. Legally, most bonds must first be approved by the Securities and Exchange Commission (SEC). (The SEC is a government entity that regulates the sale of all public securities.) The investment bankers guide the company through the SEC approval process, and then market the offering utilizing a written prospectus, its sales force and a roadshow to find investors.

The question of equity

Investment banks underwrite share (stock) offerings as well as bond offerings. In Europe, arrangements for share offerings differ between national jurisdictions. In the share offering

Visit **Vault Europe's Finance Career Channel** at www.Vault.com/Europe for insider firm profiles, employee surveys of banking profesionals in Europe, job listings, expert finance career advice, insider salary information and more.

VAULT CAREER LIBRARY

11

process, a company sells a portion of the **equity** (or ownership) of itself to the investing public. The very first time a company chooses to sell equity, this offering of equity is transacted through a process called an initial public offering of stock (commonly known as an IPO). Through the IPO process, stock in a company is created and sold to the public. After the deal, stock sold in the U.S. is traded on a stock exchange such as the New York Stock Exchange (NYSE) or the Nasdaq. In Europe, shares issued in the UK are traded on the London Stock Exchange, in Germany on the Deutsche Borse and in France on Euronext. We will cover the equity offering process in greater detail in Chapter 6. The equity underwriting process is another major way in which investment banking differs from commercial banking.

US commercial banks and European universal banks underwrite debt issues, and some have substantial expertise in underwriting public bond deals. So, not only do these banks make loans utilizing their deposits, they also underwrite bonds through a corporate finance department. When it comes to underwriting bond offerings, commercial banks have long competed for this business directly with investment banks. However, as a practical matter, only the biggest tier of commercial banks are able to do so, because the size of most public bond issues is large and competition from the major investment banks for such deals is very fierce.

Development of Investment Banking in London

London and New York are the world's leading international financial centres and the twin the capitals of the investment banking industry. Both serve global, regional, and domestic clients. New York is the foremost U.S. domestic financial centre and regional centre for the Americas. London is the primary investment banking centre for the European Union as well as for the UK market.

Among European financial centres, London ranks far ahead of Frankfurt and Paris, its nearest rivals. An extensive study of financial centre competitiveness across a range of key variables in 2003 produced the following: London — 3.71; Paris — 2.99; and Frankfurt — 2.81. In 2005, no less than half of total European investment banking activity was conducted through London. Its leading position is the result of the unrivalled depth of its specialist labour market, its trading culture, the use of English as the language of international finance, the effectiveness of its regulatory arrangements, its relatively attractive taxation levels, and a long-standing tradition of openness and internationalism.

The district in which banks and other financial services firms traditionally clustered is called "the City." It is the oldest part of London and was originally surrounded by the city wall — hence its name. The City continues to be the main financial area: it is location of the Bank of England, the London Stock Exchange, the Lloyd's of London insurance market and other important institutions, and of many banks.

The development of a second financial services cluster at Canary Wharf, about three miles east of the City, began in the late 1980s. Frustrated by the high cost of office rents and zoning restrictions on new developments because of the area's historic ties, the London head of investment bank Credit Suisse First Boston put together a consortium that developed a new purpose-built complex on the site of derelict docks. The first building at Canary Wharf opened in the early 1990s and today around 80,000 people work in the ever-expanding office and retail complex. Many of the leading players in investment banking have relocated their London headquarters to state-of-the-art buildings at Canary Wharf.

Investment banking activities, such as bond issues, have been undertaken in London for more than two centuries — even longer than New York. The business was undertaken by a set of specialist firms known as merchant banks. Although in Europe there has never been a regulatory prohibition on commercial banks undertaking investment banking activities — no equivalent of the U.S Glass-Steagall Act — it was not until the 1980s that UK commercial banks began to undertake investment banking business. In continental Europe, however, the major banks have always provided investment banking services to their corporate clients along with commercial banking services, a business model known as 'universal banking.'

In the 1990s, U.S. investment banks expanded the scale of their operations in London to participate in European economic integration, as did some U.S. commercial banks that were forbidden from doing so at home because of Glass-Steagall regulatory restrictions. At the same time, some of the British and major Continental European universal banks decided to develop their international investment banking activities, which also meant developing a greater presence in London. The quickest way to do so was by buying one of the independent British merchant banks, which largely disappeared as a result.

The outcome of these developments was some fundamental shifts in the ownership pattern and structure of the investment banking industry in London. Today there are four principal types of participant: (1) U.S. 'pure' investment banks, notably Goldman Sachs, Merrill Lynch, Morgan Stanley and Lehman Brothers; (2) U.S. universal banks, notably Citigroup and JP Morgan; (3) UK and European universal banks, notably HSBC, Barclays, Royal Bank of Scotland, Deutsche Bank, UBS, Credit Suisse, ABN Amro, BNP Paribas, Societe Generale, ING and Dresdner; and (4) a number of specialist independents, such as Rothschild, Lazards and Close Brothers.

Visit **Vault Europe's Finance Career Channel** at www.Vault.com/Europe for insider firm profiles, employee surveys of banking profesionals in Europe, job listings, expert finance career advice, insider salary information and more.

VAULT CAREER LIBRARY 13

Hedge Funds: What Exactly Are They?

Hedge funds are one sexy component of the buy side. Since the mid-1990s, hedge funds' popularity has grown tremendously. Hedge funds pool together money from large investors (usually wealthy individuals) with the goal of making outsized gains. Historically, hedge funds bought individual stocks, and shorted (or borrowed against) the S&P 500, FT 100 or another market index, as a hedge against the stock. (The funds bet against the market index in order to reduce their risk.) As long as the individual stocks outperformed the market index, the fund made money.

Nowadays, hedge funds have evolved into a myriad of high-risk money managers who essentially borrow money to invest in a multitude of stocks, bonds and derivative instruments (these funds with borrowed money are said to be leveraged).

Essentially, a hedge fund uses its equity base to borrow substantially more capital, and therefore multiply its returns through this risky leveraging. Buying derivatives is a common way to quickly leverage a portfolio. Because hedge funds have relatively few (and wealthy) shareholders, they remain largely unregulated.

The Buy-Side vs. the Sell-Side

The traditional investment banking world is considered the "sell-side" of the securities industry. Why? Investment banks create stocks and bonds, and sell these securities to investors. Sell is the key word, as I-banks continually sell their firms' capabilities to generate corporate finance business, and salespeople sell securities to generate commission revenue.

Who are the buyers ("buy-side") of public stocks and bonds? They are individual investors (you and me) and institutional investors: collectively managed funds such as mutual funds in the U.S. and OEICs (Open-Ended Investment Companies) in the European Union; charities; private company and public sector pension funds. The universe of institutional investors is appropriately called the buy-side of the securities industry.

Mutual fund companies, such as Fidelity and Vanguard in the U.S., Schroders and M&G Group in the UK, now represent a large portion of buy-side business. Insurance companies like Prudential and Northwestern Mutual in the U.S. and Prudential and Legal & General in the UK also manage large blocks of assets and are another segment of the buy-side. Yet another class of buy-side firms manage pension fund assets — frequently, a company's pension assets will be given to a specialty buy-side firm that can better manage the funds and hopefully generate higher returns than the company itself could have. There is substantial overlap among these money managers — some, such as Putnam and T. Rowe, manage both mutual funds for individuals as well as pension fund assets of large corporations.

Visit **Vault Europe's Finance Career Channel** at **www.Vault.com/Europe** for insider firm profiles, employee surveys of banking profesionals in Europe, job listings, expert finance career advice, insider salary information and more.

VAULT CAREER LIBRARY   15

The Equity Markets

CHAPTER 3

"The FTSE 100 gave up early gains to finish 10.7 points, or 0.2 per cent, lower at 5,818.1. However, the FTSE 250 put on 13.7 points, or 0.2 per cent to 9,299.6," the *Financial Times* reported on August 9, 2006. "The majority of the FTSE 100's fall was down to BP, 1.4 per cent lower at 614p, which knocked 1.4 per cent off the main index...The FTSE Eurofirst 300 ended 0.1 per cent higher at 1,330.84 as gains for financial heavyweights offset losses for oil stocks."

If you are new to the financial industry, you may be wondering exactly what all of these headlines mean and how to interpret them. The next two chapters are intended to provide a quick overview of the financial markets and what drives them, and introduce you to some market lingo as well. For reference, many definitions and explanations of many common types of securities can be found in the glossary at the end of this guide.

Bears vs. Bulls

Almost everyone loves a bull market, and an investor seemingly cannot go wrong when the market continues to reach new highs. At Goldman Sachs, a bull market is said to occur when stocks exhibit expanding multiples — we will give you a simpler definition. Essentially, a bull market occurs when the price of stocks — also called **shares** in Europe — move up (as measured by an index like the FTSE 100 or the FTSE Eurofirst 300). A **bear market** occurs when shares fall. Simple. More specifically, bear markets generally occur when the market has fallen by greater than 20 percent from its highs, and a correction occurs when the market has fallen by more than 10 percent but less than 20 percent.

Stock market indices

A stock market index provides a statistical summary of the value of the component stocks/shares. They are used to monitor the direction of share price movements in the market as a whole, or some component element or sector, and as benchmarks for investment products and the performance of investment portfolios. The most widely publicised, most widely traded, and most widely tracked stock index in the world is the **Dow Jones Industrial Average**, created in 1896. The Dow Jones is composed of 30 major U.S. companies. The **Standard and Poor's 500 Index** (S&P 500) provides a broader based

Visit **Vault Europe's Finance Career Channel** at **www.Vault.com/Europe** for insider firm profiles, employee surveys of banking profesionals in Europe, job listings, expert finance career advice, insider salary information and more.

VAULT CAREER LIBRARY 17

yardstick of the US stock prices. The other major U.S. stock market index is the **Nasdaq Composite** that reflects the prices of stocks quoted on the Nasdaq electronic stock market.

UK stock market indices

The **FTSE 100** (called the *footsie*) is the leading price index for UK shares. Introduced in 1984, the Financial Times-Stock Exchange 100 Index comprises the 100 most highly capitalised UK companies — known as 'large-caps' or 'blue chips' — representing around 80 percent of the UK share market. It is regarded as a barometer for the UK economy and is the foremost European share index. A variety of investment products, such as derivatives and exchange-traded funds, are based on the FTSE 100. The make-up of the index is determined quarterly among companies with a full listing on the London Stock Exchange. The threshold for inclusion at the start of 2006 was around £2 billion. BP had the largest market capitalisation — £128 billion. The rest of the top ten constituents were: Royal Dutch Shell, HSBC, GlaxoSmithKline, Vodafone, Royal Bank of Scotland, AstraZeneca, Barclays, HBOS and Anglo American. Trading in FTSE 100 company shares comprises around 85 percent of UK share trading turnover.

The FTSE 100 is produced by the FTSE Group, originally a joint venture between the Financial Times newspaper and the London Stock Exchange but now an independent specialist company that calculates over 100,000 indices covering around 50 counties and all major asset classes. The longest-running UK share index is the FT30 that has been calculated since 1935. Today, however, it is only used only to make very long-term comparisons. The other leading UK indices are the:

- **FTSE 250 Index** — the constituents are the 250 next biggest companies — the so-called 'mid-caps' — and represents about 17 percent of the aggregate market capitalisation of the London Stock Exchange.

- **FTSE 350 Index** — an aggregation of the FTSE 100 and FTSE 250 indices.

- **FTSE SmallCap Index** — comprises companies smaller that those included in the FTSE 350 Index, amounting to around 2 percent of the UK market.

- **FTSE All-Share Index** — comprises the largest 800 or so UK companies that account for some 98 per cent of UK market capitalisation. It is a key benchmark for asset managers — the principal yardstick against which their performance is rated.

As the market report from the *Financial Times* at the start of this chapter demonstrated, it is possible for different indices to move in different directions on the same day. That is

VAULT CAREER LIBRARY

because they measure different parts of the market that are driven by different factors — well, up to a point.

Some 2,500 UK companies and 350 overseas companies are listed on the London Stock Exchange. Around 1,200 companies that are too small or too new to meet the listing criteria of the senior market may list on the Alternative Investment Market (AIM). This junior market, created in 1995 and run by the London Stock Exchange, is designed to meet the requirements of young and growing companies often based on new technologies. The most successful AIM companies migrate to the main market. The AIM market is covered by a range of FTSE indices, notably the:

- **FTSE AIM 50 Index** — comprises the largest 50 AIM-listed companies

- **FTSE AIM 100 Index** — comprises the largest 100 AIM-listed companies

- **FTSE AIM All-Share Index** — covers the whole AIM market

European stock market indices

The **DAX Index** is the leading share index for German companies, being composed of 30 of the largest companies listed on the Frankfurt Stock Exchange. The **CAC 40 Index** comprises 40 major French companies whose shares are quoted on the Euronext Paris stock exchange.

The FTSEEurofirst Index Series is a range of Europe-wide share indexes that are a joint product of the FTSE Group and Euronext, the operator of the Amsterdam, Brussels, Paris and Lisbon stock exchanges and LIFFE, the London International Financial Futures and Options Exchange. The series includes:

- **FTSEEurofirst 80 Index** — comprises the 60 largest quoted European companies by market capitalisation plus 20 additional companies chosen for their size and sector representation.

- **FTSEEurofirst 100 Index** — comprises the 60 largest quoted companies by market capitalisation in the FTSE Developed Europe Index plus 40 additional companies selected on the basis of size and sector representation.

- **FTSEEurofirst 300 Index** — comprises the 300 largest European quoted companies by market capitalisation.

sit **Vault Europe's Finance Career Channel** at **www.Vault.com/Europe** for insider firm ofiles, employee surveys of banking profesionals in Europe, job listings, expert finance reer advice, insider salary information and more.

VAULT CAREER LIBRARY 19

Big-cap and small-cap

At a basic level, market capitalization or market cap represents the company's value according to the market, and is calculated by multiplying the total number of shares by share price. (This is the equity value of the company.) Companies and their stocks tend to be categorized into three broad categories: big-cap, mid-cap and small-cap.

While there are no hard and fast rules, generally speaking in the UK, a company with a market cap greater than £2 billion will be classified as a big-cap stock. These companies tend to be established, mature companies, although this is not necessarily the case. Sometimes huge companies, for example the U.S. corporations GE and Microsoft, are called mega-cap stocks. Small-cap stocks tend to be riskier, but are also often the faster growing companies. Roughly speaking, a small-cap stock includes those companies with market caps less than £100 million. As one might expect, the stocks in between £100 million and £2 billion are referred to as mid-cap stocks.

What moves the stock market?

Not surprisingly, the factors that most influence the broader stock market are economic in nature. Among equities, corporate profits and the interest rates are king.

Corporate profits: When Gross Domestic Product slows substantially, market investors fear a recession and a drop in corporate profits. And if economic conditions worsen and the market enters a recession, many companies will face reduced demand for their products, company earnings will be hurt, and hence equity (stock) prices will decline. Thus, when the GDP suffers, so does the stock market.

Interest rates: When the Consumer Price Index heats up, investors fear inflation. **Inflation** fears trigger a different chain of events than fears of recession. Most importantly, inflation will cause interest rates to rise. Companies with debt will be forced to pay higher interest rates on existing debt, thereby reducing earnings (and earnings per share). And compounding the problem, because inflation fears cause interest rates to rise, higher rates will make investments other than stocks more attractive from the investor's perspective. Why would an investor purchase a stock that may only earn 8 percent (and carries substantial risk), when lower risk CD's and government bonds offer similar yields with less risk? These inflation fears are known as capital allocations in the market (whether investors are putting money into stocks vs. bonds), which can substantially impact stock and bond prices. Investors typically re-allocate funds from stocks to low-risk bonds when the economy experiences a slowdown and vice versa when the opposite occurs.

What moves *individual* stocks?

When it comes to individual stocks, it's all about earnings, earnings, earnings. No other measure even compares to **earnings per share** (EPS) when it comes to an individual stock's price. Every quarter, public companies must report EPS figures, and stockholders wait with bated breath, ready to compare the actual EPS figure with the EPS estimates set by City research analysts. For instance, if a company reports £1.00 EPS for a quarter, but the market had anticipated EPS of £1.20, then the stock will almost certainly be dramatically hit in the market the next trading day. Conversely, a company that beats its estimates will typically rally in the markets.

It is important to note at this point, that in the frenzied Internet stock market of 1999 and early 2000, investors did not show the traditional focus on near-term earnings. It was acceptable for these companies to operate at a loss for a year or more, because these companies, investors hoped, would achieve long term future earnings. However, when the markets turned in the spring of 2000 investors began to expect even "new economy" companies to demonstrate more substantial near-term earnings capacity.

The market does not care about last year's earnings or even last quarter's earnings. What matters most is what will happen in the near future. Investors maintain a tough, "what have you done for me lately" attitude, and forgive slowly a company that consistently fails to meet analysts' estimates ("misses its numbers").

sit **Vault Europe's Finance Career Channel** at **www.Vault.com/Europe** for insider firm
ofiles, employee surveys of banking profesionals in Europe, job listings, expert finance
reer advice, insider salary information and more.

V∧ULT CAREER
LIBRARY   **21**

Stock Valuation Measures and Ratios

As far as stocks go, it is important to realize that absolute stock prices mean nothing. A £100 stock could be "cheaper" than a £10 stock. To clarify how this works, consider the following ratios and what they mean. Keep in mind that these are only a few of the major ratios, and that literally hundreds of financial and accounting ratios have been invented to compare dissimilar companies. Again, it is important to note that most of these ratios were not as applicable in the market's recent evaluation of certain Internet and technology stocks.

P/E ratio

You can't go far into a discussion about the stock market without hearing about the all-important **price to earnings ratio**, or P/E ratio. By definition, a P/E ratio equals the stock price divided by the earnings per share. In usage, investors use the P/E ratio to indicate how cheap or expensive a stock is.

Consider the following example. Two similar firms each have £1.50 in EPS. Company A's stock price is £15.00 per share, and Company B's stock price is £30.00 per share.

Company	Stock Price	Earnings Per Share	P/E Ratio
A	£15.00	£1.50	10x
B	£30.00	£1.50	20x

Clearly, Company A is cheaper than Company B with regard to the P/E ratio because both firms exhibit the same level of earnings, but A's stock trades at a higher price. That is, Company A's P/E ratio of 10 (15/1.5) is lower than Company B's P/E ratio of 20 (30/1.5). Hence, Company A's stock trades at a lower price. The terminology one hears in the market is, "Company A is trading at 10 times earnings, while Company B is trading at 20 times earnings." Twenty times is a higher multiple.

However, the true measure of cheapness vs. richness cannot be summed up by the P/E ratio. Some firms simply deserve higher P/E ratios than others, and some deserve lower P/Es. Importantly, the distinguishing factor is the anticipated growth in earnings per share.

Vault Career Guide to Investment Banking • European Edition

The Equity Markets

PEG ratio

Because companies grow at different rates, another comparison investors often make is between the P/E ratio and the stock's expected growth rate in EPS. Returning to our previous example, let's say Company A has an expected EPS growth rate of 10 percent, while Company B's expected growth rate is 20 percent.

Company	Stock Price	Earnings Per Share	P/E Ratio	Estimated Growth Rate in EPS
A	£15.00	£1.50	10x	10x
B	£30.00	£1.50	20x	20x

We might propose that the market values Company A at 10 times earnings because it anticipates 10 percent annual growth in EPS over the next five years. Company B is growing faster — at a 20 percent rate — and therefore justifies the 20 times earnings stock price. To determine true cheapness, market analysts have developed a ratio that compares the P/E to the growth rate — the **PEG ratio**. In this example, one could argue that both companies are priced similarly (both have PEG ratios of 1).

Sophisticated market investors therefore utilize this PEG ratio rather than just the P/E ratio. Roughly speaking, the average company has a PEG ratio of 1:1 or 1 (i.e., the P/E ratio matches the anticipated growth rate). By convention, "expensive" firms have a PEG ratio greater than one, and "cheap" stocks have a PEG ratio less than one.

Cash flow multiples

For companies with no earnings (or losses) and therefore no EPS (or negative EPS), one cannot calculate the P/E ratio — it is a meaningless number. An alternative is to compute the firm's cash flow and compare that to the market value of the firm. The following example illustrates how a typical cash flow multiple like Enterprise Value/EBITDA ratio is calculated.

EBITDA: A proxy for cash flow, EBITDA stands for Earnings Before Interest, Taxes, Depreciation and Amortization. To calculate EBITDA, work your way up the Income Statement, adding back the appropriate items to net income. (Note: For a more detailed explanation of this and other financial caculations, see the *Vault Guide to Finance Interviews*.) Adding together depreciation and amortization to operating earnings, a common subtotal on the income statement, can serve as a shortcut to calculating EBITDA.

sit **Vault Europe's Finance Career Channel** at www.Vault.com/Europe for insider firm ofiles, employee surveys of banking profesionals in Europe, job listings, expert finance reer advice, insider salary information and more.

VAULT CAREER LIBRARY 23

Enterprise value (EV) = market value of equity + net debt. To compute market value of equity, simply multiply the current stock price times the number of shares outstanding. Net debt is simply the firm's total debt (as found on the balance sheet) minus cash.

Enterprise value to revenue multiple (EV/revenue)

If you follow startup companies or young technology or healthcare related companies, you have probably heard the multiple of revenue lingo. Sometimes it is called the price-sales ratio (though this technically is not correct). Why use this ratio? For one, many firms not only have negative earnings, but also negative cash flow. That means any cash flow or P/E multiple must be thrown out the window, leaving revenue as the last positive income statement number left to compare to the firm's enterprise value. Specifically one calculates this ratio by dividing EV by the last 12 months revenue figure.

Return on equity (ROE)

ROE = Net income divided by total shareholders equity. An important measure, especially for financial services companies, that evaluates the income return that a firm earned in any given year. Return on equity is expressed as a percentage. Many firms' financial goal is to achieve a certain level of ROE per year, say 20 percent or more.

Value Stocks, Growth Stocks and Momentum Investors

It is important to know that investors typically classify stocks into one of two categories — growth and value stocks. Momentum investors buy a subset of the stocks in the growth category.

Value stocks are those that often have been battered by investors. Typically, a stock that trades at low P/E ratios after having once traded at high P/E's, or a stock with declining sales or earnings fits into the value category. Investors choose value stocks with the hope that their businesses will turn around and profits will return. Or, investors perhaps realize that a stock is trading close to or even below its "break-up value" (net proceeds upon liquidation of the company), and hence have little downside.

Growth stocks are just the opposite. High P/E's, high growth rates, and often hot stocks fit the growth category. Technology stocks, with sometimes astoundingly high P/E's, may be classified as growth stocks, based on their high growth potential. Keep in mind that a P/E ratio often serves as a proxy for a firm's average expected growth rate, because as discussed, investors will generally pay a high P/E for a faster growing company.

Momentum investors buy growth stocks that have exhibited strong upward price appreciation. Usually trading at or near their "52-week highs" (the highest trading price during the previous two weeks), momentum investors cause these stocks to trade up and down with extreme volatility. Momentum investors, who typically don't care much about the firm's business or valuation ratios, will dump their stocks the moment they show price weakness. Thus, a stock run-up by momentum investors can potentially crash dramatically as they bail out at the first sign of trouble.

Basic Equity Definitions

Ordinary shares (UK)/common stock (U.S.)/equity: Ownership of ordinary shares confers part ownership of the issuing company and rights to vote and receive dividends. The vast majority of shares traded in the markets is ordinary shares.

Preference shares (UK)/preferred stock (U.S.): provide shareholders with a first claim on dividends and on the company's assets in case of liquidation. As an asset class, preference shares are a halfway house between fixed-rate bonds and ordinary shares. There are several types of preference share

Visit **Vault Europe's Finance Career Channel** at www.Vault.com/Europe for insider firm profiles, employee surveys of banking profesionals in Europe, job listings, expert finance career advice, insider salary information and more.

VAULT CAREER LIBRARY 25

designed to meet companies' financing requirements and to appeal to investors who are apprehensive about the risks of ordinary shares. **Redeemable preference shares** have a guarantee of repayment by the company at a future date. **Participating preference shares** pay a lower basic dividend but if the ordinary dividend is high holders participate in the company's success through a bonus. **Convertible preference shares** allow holders to convert into ordinary shares, providing the opportunity of future gains.

The Fixed Income Markets

CHAPTER 4

What is the Bond Market?

What is the bond market? The average person doesn't follow it and often doesn't even hear very much about it. Because of the bond market's low profile, it's surprising to many people that the bond markets are even larger than the equity markets.

The total outstanding value of the global bond market in 2005 was around $60 trillion — twice the size of a decade earlier. The U.S. is the largest market for bonds with 40 percent of global outstanding value. Next are Japan with 15 percent, Germany with 7 percent and the UK with 5 percent.

U.S. bond markets

The biggest borrower of all is the U.S. government — U.S. Treasury securities constitute the world's largest asset class. U.S. Treasuries have the highest credit-rating of all bonds, investors taking the view that a default by the U.S. is inconceivable (and if it ever happened, the world financial market would essentially be in shambles). Because they are virtually risk-free U.S. Treasuries offer relatively low yields (a low rate of interest) which provides a market benchmark for the pricing of the bonds of other borrowers.

Further important components of the U.S. bond market are:

- Agency bonds
- High grade corporate bonds
- High yield (junk) bonds
- Municipal bonds
- Mortgage-backed bonds
- Asset-backed securities

UK bond markets

The outstanding value of the UK bond market in 2005 was around $3 trillion. The largest borrower is the UK government, whose bonds, known as gilts, comprise around a fifth of outstanding value. There is a very active market in gilts, dealing being handled by 16 major I-banks and commercial banks registered as Gilt-Edged Market Makers (GEMMS). Other

isit **Vault Europe's Finance Career Channel** at www.Vault.com/Europe for insider firm rofiles, employee surveys of banking profesionals in Europe, job listings, expert finance areer advice, insider salary information and more.

VAULT CAREER LIBRARY 27

UK fixed interest securities include convertible and preference shares, and bonds issues by companies, banks and local authorities. Traditionally UK companies have raised debt finance from banks so the corporate bond market is relatively small — but it is growing fast.

International bonds

London is the world's foremost centre for the issuance and trading of international bonds, the bulk of which are **eurobonds** — bonds issued by a borrower in a currency other than its domestic currency (in London usually dollars or yen or Deutsche marks). It is estimated that 60 percent of eurobond primary issuance and 70 percent of secondary market trading is conducted in London and these activities are main reasons for London's importance as an I-banking and international financial centre.

Bond Market Indicators

The yield curve

Bond **"yields"** are the current rate of return to an investor who buys the bond. (Yield is measured in **"basis points"**; each basis point = 1/100 of one percent.) A primary measure of importance to fixed income investors is the yield curve. The **yield curve** (also called the "term structure of interest rates") depicts graphically the yields on different maturity U.S. government securities. To construct a simple yield curve, investors typically look at the yield on a 90-day U.S. T-bill and then the yield on the 30-year U.S. government bond (called the Long Bond). Typically, the yields of shorter-term government T-bill are lower than Long Bond's yield, indicating what is called an **"upward sloping yield curve."** Sometimes, short-term interest rates are higher than long-term rates, creating what is known as an **"inverse yield curve."**

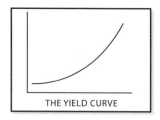

THE YIELD CURVE

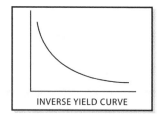

INVERSE YIELD CURVE

Bond indices

As with the stock market, the bond market has some widely watched indexes of its own. One prominent example is the Lehman Government Corporate Bond Index ("LGC"). The LGC index measures the returns on mostly government securities, but also blends in a portion of corporate bonds. The index is adjusted periodically to reflect the percentage of assets in government and in corporate bonds in the market. Mortgage bonds are excluded entirely from the LGC index.

Spreads

In the bond world, investors track "spreads" as carefully as any single index of bond prices or any single bond. The spread is essentially the difference between a bond's yield (the amount of interest, measured in percent, paid to bondholders), and the yield on a U.S. Treasury bond of the same time to maturity. For instance, an investor investigating the 20-year Acme Corp. bond would compare it to a U.S. Treasury bond that has 20 years remaining until maturity. Because U.S. Treasury bonds are considered to have zero risk of default, a corporation's bond will always trade at a yield that is over the yield on a comparable Treasury bond. For example, if the Acme Corp. 10-year bond traded at a yield of 8.4 percent and a 10-year Treasury note was trading at 8 percent, a trader would say that the Acme bond was trading at "40 over" (here, the "40" refers to 40 basis points).

Bond ratings for corporate and municipal bonds

A bond's risk level, or the risk that the bond issuer will default on payments to bondholders, is measured by bond rating agencies. Several companies rate credit, but Standard & Poor's and Moody's are the two largest. The riskier a bond, the larger the spread: low-risk bonds trade at a small spread to Treasuries, while below-investment grade bonds trade at tremendous spreads to Treasuries. Investors refer to company specific risk as credit risk.

Triple A ratings represents the highest possible corporate bond designation, and are reserved for the best-managed, largest blue-chip companies. Triple A bonds trade at a yield close to the yield on a risk-free government Treasury. Junk bonds, or bonds with a rating of BB or below on the S&P scale, currently trade at yields ranging from 10 to 15 percent, depending on the precise rating and government bond interest rates at the time.

Companies continue to be monitored by the rating agencies as long as their bonds trade in the markets. If a company is put on "credit watch," it is possible that the rating agencies are considering raising or lowering the rating on the company. Often an agency will put a company's bonds on credit watch "with postive or negative implications," giving investors

Visit **Vault Europe's Finance Career Channel** at www.Vault.com/Europe for insider firm profiles, employee surveys of banking profesionals in Europe, job listings, expert finance career advice, insider salary information and more.

VAULT CAREER LIBRARY 29

a preview of which way any future change will go. When a bond is actually downgraded by Moody's or S&P, the bond's price drops dramatically (and therefore its yield increases).

The following table summarizes rating symbols of the two major rating agencies and provides a brief definition of each.

Bond Rating Codes

Rating	S&P	Moody's
Highest quality	AAA	Aaa
High quality	AA	Aa
Upper medium quality	A	A
Medium grade	BBB	Baa
Somewhat speculative	BB	Ba
Low grade, speculative	B	B
Low grade, default possible	CCC	Caa
Low grade, partial recovery possible	CC	Ca
Default expected	C	C

Source: Moody's Investor's Service and Standard and Poor's

Factors affecting the bond market

What factors affect the bond market? In short, **interest rates**. The general level of interest rates, as measured by many different barometers (see inset) moves bond prices up and down, in dramatic inverse fashion. In other words, if interest rates rise, the bond markets suffer.

Think of it this way. Say you own a bond that is paying you a fixed rate of 8 percent today, and that this rate represents a 1.5 percent spread over Treasuries. An increase in rates of 1 percent means that this same bond purchased now (as opposed to when you purchased the bond) will now yield 9 percent. And as the yield goes up, the price declines. So, your bond loses value and you are only earning 8 percent when the rest of the market is earning 9 percent.

You could have waited, purchased the bond after the rate increase, and earned a greater yield. The opposite occurs when rates go down. If you lock in a fixed rate of 8 percent and rates plunge by 1 percent, you now earn more than those who purchase the bond after the rate decrease. Therefore, as interest rates change the price or value of bonds will rise or fall so that all comparaqble bonds will trade at the same yield regardless of when or at what interest rate these bonds were issued.

Which Interest Rate Are You Talking About?

Investment banking professionals often discuss interest rates in general terms. But what are they really talking about? So many rates are tossed about that they may be difficult to track. To clarify, we will take a brief look at the key rates worth tracking. We have ranked them in typically ascending order: the discount rate usually is the lowest rate; the yield on junk bonds is usually the highest.

The discount rate: The discount rate is the rate that the Federal Reserve charges on overnight loans to banks. Today, the discount rate can be directly changed by the Fed, but maintains a largely symbolic role.

Federal funds rate: The rate domestic banks charge one another on overnight loans to meet Federal Reserve requirements. This rate is also directly controlled by the Fed and is a critical interest rate to financial markets.

T-Bill yields: The yield or internal rate of return an investor would receive at any given moment on a 90- to 360-day Treasury bill.

LIBOR (London Interbank Offered Rate): The wholesale rate banks active in the London eurocurrency market charge one another on overnight loans or loans up to five years. Often used by banks to quote floating rate loan interest rates. Typically, the benchmark LIBOR used on loans is the three-month rate.

The Long Bond (30-Year Treasury) yield: The yield or internal rate of return an investor would receive at any given moment on the 30-year U.S. Treasury bond.

Municipal bond yields: The yield or internal rate of return an investor would receive at any given moment by investing in municipal bonds. We should note that the interest on municipal bonds typically is free from federal government taxes and therefore has a lower yield than other bonds of similar risk. These yields, however, can vary substantially depending on their rating, so could be higher or lower than presented here.

High grade corporate bond yield: The yield or internal rate of return an investor would receive by purchasing a corporate bond with a rating above BB.

Visit **Vault Europe's Finance Career Channel** at **www.Vault.com/Europe** for insider firm profiles, employee surveys of banking profesionals in Europe, job listings, expert finance career advice, insider salary information and more.

VAULT CAREER LIBRARY 31

Prime rate: The average rate that U.S. banks charge to companies for loans.

30-year mortgage rates: The average interest rate on 30-year home mortgages. Mortgage rates typically move in line with the yield on the 10-year Treasury note

High yield bonds: The yield or internal rate of return an investor would receive by purchasing a corporate bond with a rating below BBB (also called junk bonds).

Why do interest rates move?

Interest rates react mostly to **inflation** expectations (expectations of a rise in prices). If it is believed that inflation will rise, then interest rates rise. Think of it this way. Say inflation is 5 percent a year. In order to make money on a loan, a bank would have to at least charge more than 5 percent — otherwise it would essentially be losing money on the loan. The same is true with bonds and other fixed income products.

In the late 1970s, interest rates topped 20 percent, as inflation began to spiral out of control (and the market expected continued high inflation). Today, many believe that the Federal Reserve has successfully slayed inflation and has all but eliminated market concerns of future inflation, at least in the near term. This is certainly debatable, but clearly, the sound monetary policies and remarkable price stability in the U.S. have made it the envy of the world.

A Note About the Federal Reserve

The Federal Reserve Bank in the United States monitors the U.S. money supply and regulates banking institutions. The Fed's role is crucial to the U.S. economy and stock market.

Academic studies of economic history have shown that a country's inflation rate tends to track that country's increase in its money supply. Therefore, if the Fed allows the money supply to increase by 2 percent this year, inflation can best be predicted to increase by about 2 percent as well. And because inflation so dramatically impacts the stock and bond markets, the markets scrutinize the daily activities of the Fed and hang onto every word uttered by the Fed chairman.

The Fed can manage consumption patterns and hence the GDP by raising or lowering interest rates.

The chain of events when the Fed raises rates is as follows:

The Fed raises interest rates. This interest rate increase triggers banks to raise interest rates, which leads to consumers and businesses borrowing less and spending less. This decrease in consumption tends to slow down GDP, thereby reducing earnings at companies. Since consumers and businesses borrow less, they have left their money in the bank and hence the money supply does not expand. Note also that since companies tend to borrow less when rates go up, they therefore typically invest less in capital equipment, which discourages productivity gains and hurts earnings of capital goods providers. Any economist will tell you that a key to a growing economy on a per capita basis is improving labor productivity.

Fixed Income Definitions

The following glossary may be useful for defining securities that trade in the markets as well as talking about the factors that influence them. Note that this is just a list of the most common types of fixed income products and economic indicators. Thousands of fixed income products actually trade in the markets.

Types of Securities	
Treasury securities	United States government-issued securities. Categorized as Treasury bills (maturity of up to — but not including — two years), Treasury notes (from two years to 10 years maturity), and Treasury bonds (10 years to 30 years). As they are government-guaranteed, Treasuries are considered "risk-free." In fact, U.S. Treasuries have no default risk, but do have interest rate risk — if rates increase, then the price of US Treasuries issued in the past will decrease.
Agency bonds	Agencies represent all bonds issued by the federal government and federal agencies, but excluding those issued by the Treasury (i.e., bonds issued by other agencies of the federal government). Examples of agencies that issue bonds include Federal National Mortgage Association (FNMA) and Guaranteed National Mortgage Association (GNMA).

Visit **Vault Europe's Finance Career Channel** at **www.Vault.com/Europe** for insider firm profiles, employee surveys of banking profesionals in Europe, job listings, expert finance career advice, insider salary information and more.

VAULT CAREER LIBRARY

33

Types of Securities	
Investment grade corporate bonds	Bonds with a Standard & Poor's rating of at least a BBB-. Typically big, blue-chip companies issue highly rated bonds.
High yield (junk) bonds	Bonds with a Standard & Poor's rating lower than BBB-. Typically smaller, riskier companies issue high yield bonds.
Money market securities	The market for securities (typically corporate, but also Treasury securities) maturing within one year, including short-term CDs, Repurchase Agreements, and Commercial Paper (low-risk corporate issues), among others. These are low-risk, short-term securities that have yields similar to Treasuries.
Mortgage-backed bonds	Bonds collateralized by a pool of mortgages. Interest and principal payments are based on the individual homeowners making their mortgage payments. The more diverse the pool of mortgages backing the bond, the less risky they are typically considered.

Economic Indicators	
Gross Domestic Product	GDP measures the total domestic output of goods and services in the United States. Generally, when the GDP grows at a rate of less than 2%, the economy is considered to be in an economic slowdown; negative growth, or shrinkage, indicates recession.
Consumer Price Index	The CPI measures the percentage increase in the price for goods and services. Essentially, the CPI measures inflation affecting consumers.
Producer Price Index	The PPI measures the percentage increase in the price of a standard basket of goods and services. PPI is a measure of inflation for producers and manufacturers.
Unemployment Rate and Wages	In 1999 through early 2000, U.S. unemployment was at record lows. Clearly, this was a positive sign for the U.S. economy because jobs are plentiful. The markets sometimes react negatively to extremely low levels of unemployment, since, as a tight labor market means that firms may have to raise wages (called wage pressure). Substantial wage pressure may force firms to raise prices, and hence may cause inflation to flare up. Marked increases in unemployment are seen as a sign of economic weakness, and can be a symptom of a slowdown or recession.

Trends in the Investment Banking Industry

CHAPTER 5

Recent Developments in I-Banking

Global investment banking fee revenues increased by 14 percent in 2005, and continued to head north in the first half of 2006. It was the third year of expansion for the industry, following the downturn in revenues between 2000 and 2002 due to an economic slowdown and falls in equity markets. According to consultants Freeman & Co., in 2005 global investment banking revenues were $52 billion, up from $34 billion in 2002 and only 7 percent below the 2000 peak.

The U.S. was, as ever, the largest source of investment banking fee revenues, 51 percent of the total coming from the Americas. Europe (plus the Middle East and Africa) were the source of 31 percent, and Asia 18 percent. The trends over the past decade have been for the proportionate contribution of the U.S. to contract, of Asia to grow and for Europe to remain at around 30 percent. Over the years 2002 to 2005, fee income from Asia grew by 98 percent, from Europe by 55 per cent and from the U.S. by 46 percent.

The activity that generated the greatest investment banking fee income in 2005 was merger and acquisition (M&A) advisory — $24 billion, 46 percent of the total. Equity underwriting accounted for 34 percent of fee revenue, $18 billion. Fixed income underwriting produced $10 billion, 20 percent of the total.

M&A boom

Mergers and acquisition advisory has been the foremost source of global investment banking industry fee income over the past decade, generating more than two fifths of the total. However, the level of M&A business is very volatile, being affected by a variety of economic, financial and political factors. The late 1990s saw a boom in global M&A activity that peaked in 2000 in which year deals totalled almost $3.5 trillion. But in 2002 activity was down to $1.2 trillion.

A new boom in global M&A got underway in 2004, supported by rising equity prices, low interest rates, strong corporate earnings and a confident outlook. Global M&A activity in 2005 was $2.7 trillion, a 38 percent increase on the year before. The U.S. and Europe each saw deals totalling around $1 trillion, a 33 percent rise for the U.S. and a 40 percent increase for Europe. Since the mid-1990s, the proportion of activity taking place in Europe

Visit **Vault Europe's Finance Career Channel** at www.Vault.com/Europe for insider firm profiles, employee surveys of banking profesionals in Europe, job listings, expert finance career advice, insider salary information and more.

VAULT CAREER LIBRARY 35

has risen from about 10 percent to almost 40 percent. Underlying the strong growth of European M&A activity is the restructuring of industries as they shift focus from fragmented national markets to a single continent-wide European market.

Goldman Sachs topped the Thomson Financial league table for global M&A in 2005, for the eighth year running. It worked on 433 deals with an aggregate value of $867 billion, a 58 percent hike on the previous year. Morgan Stanley was second, with a deal count of 379 worth $726 billion. Third was JP Morgan, with 400 transactions worth $659 billion. The energy and financial sectors were the leading sectors for worldwide merger activity, with deals worth $416 billion and $414 billion respectively.

Goldman Sachs took the top spot in the Thomson Financial league table of European M&A in 2005, working on 190 deals with a total value of $417 billion. Second place went to JP Morgan, advising on 210 transactions worth $340 billion. The most active sectors for European M&A were energy and financials, with UK and German companies as the most sought after targets for takeovers.

A notable feature of the mid-2000s M&A boom was the major part played by financial purchasers, including some multi-billion dollar deals. Private equity groups, which are raising ever-larger funds, were buyers on an unprecedented scale. Some of the major investment banks played a significant role in this development. Management buyouts were also a thriving contributor.

Global and European M&A activity continued to surge in the first half of 2006, up 44 percent on the same period in 2005. A substantial increase for the year as a whole was predicted, perhaps beating the previous record set in 2000.

Triumph of the traders

In recent years a rising proportion of investment banks' profits has come from trading. At Goldman Sachs in the first half of 2006, trading generated 62 percent of the firm's total revenues: fixed income, currencies and commodities, 39 percent; equities, a further 23 percent.

Traditionally trading at investment banks was conducted in equities, bonds and financial derivatives. In recent years familiar derivative contracts for currency and interest rate products have been joined by racy new creations such as CDOs (collateralised debt obligations). CDOs are part of an explosion in the conversion of assets into tradeable securities: today contracts based on, for instance, future energy prices, complex baskets of currencies or the chance of a company defaulting on its debt, are readily traded on financial markets.

A further boost to trading volumes has come from the rapid expansion of hedge funds, which are particularly active traders. This new class of clients and the prime brokerage business that serves them generated around $5 billion in revenues for the investment banks in 2005, up almost 30 percent.

Not so long ago, investment banks and brokerage houses acted primarily as agents, buying and selling on behalf of clients. Today, more and more, they act as principals, using the firm's own money to make proprietary bets. The rewards for getting it right are much greater — but so are the potential risks.

The expansion of trading revenues has propelled executives who began their careers on the trading floor to top management positions. Examples include Huw Jenkins at UBS, Oswald Grubel at Credit Suisse, and Lloyd Blankfein at Goldman Sachs. Those who make the most money are getting to run the business — and manage the risks.

Investment banks have long contained two cultures — traders and advisers. It was the latter who traditionally provided firms' chief executives and chairmen. The rise of the traders has led to tensions within firms between those from the dealing room and those on the advisory side, which have contributed to the departure of a number of prominent corporate financiers to form boutique advisory firms..

The Goliaths... and the Davids

The investment banking industry is dominated by a few companies with a global presence. In the first half of 2005 the leading three investment banks — JPMorgan, Citigroup and Deutsche Bank — received between them almost a fifth of total industry revenues. The top ten major firms- seven American, three European — accounted for half of total industry revenues.

The other half investment banking industry revenues was shared among dozens of other players, including the investment banking arms of major European and Japanese banks and some long established independents, such as Rothschild, Lazards, Mediobanca and Nomura.

A phenomenon of recent years has been the creation of a new set of independent boutique investment banks, such as Greenhill, Evercore Partners, Perella Weinberg, and others. These firms have been established by former senior executives from the major houses who have decided that they would prefer to work for themselves in smaller organisations. They focus on providing advisory services to the management of major corporations responding to a demand for independent advice that has arisen as the industry's leading firms have

Visit **Vault Europe's Finance Career Channel** at www.Vault.com/Europe for insider firm profiles, employee surveys of banking profesionals in Europe, job listings, expert finance career advice, insider salary information and more.

VAULT CAREER LIBRARY   37

grown bigger and trading profits have become more important. Some corporate clients have felt neglected and have become wary of conflicts of interest on the part of their advisers.

European banking consolidation

In Europe, the major national commercial banks have traditionally provided investment banking services for their corporate clients. Up to now, this has been done on a country by country basis. The reconfiguration of the European banking industry on a pan-European basis has been long-predicted but slow in happening. Factors inhibiting cross-border deals include legal, tax, accounting and regulatory differences between European countries, as well as political interference and protectionism.

But in the last couple of years there have been signs that cross-border bank mergers — between big banks from big countries — are beginning to happen in Europe. The first of the recent mega-deals was the $17 billion bid by Banco Santander of Spain for Abbey National of the UK in 2004. The success of this transaction paved the way for others. In 2005, UniCredit of Italy acquired HBV of Germany for $22 billion, the biggest deal so far, and ABN Amro of the Netherlands bought Banca Antonveneta of Italy for $7 billion. The trend continued in 2006, BNP Paribas of France paying $11 billion for Banco del Lavoro of Italy.

It is in the former Communist counties of central Europe that have recently joined the European Union, such as Poland, Hungary and the Czech Republic, that cross-border bank consolidation has gone furthest. Since the collapse of communism and the privatisation of the region's banks, foreign banks have acquired around 80 percent of banking business. Austrian banks have been the biggest buyers, establishing a major presence in their neighbours.

Jobs and bonuses

The buoyant conditions in the investment industry since 2003 have meant more jobs and big bonuses. On Wall Street, securities industry employment in New York City rose from 160,000 in 2003 to 175,000 in mid-2006, while in London employment in wholesale financial services increased from 305,000 in 2002 to 335, 000 in 2006.

Bonuses for 2005 hit new highs on both sides of the Atlantic. In New York investment bankers collected a record $21.5 billion, beating the previous record set in 2000. The average bonus was $125,000. In London, the payout was £7.5 billion — the biggest-ever bonus bonanza, with an estimated 3,000 fortunate individuals receiving over £1 million. The highest payers were the major investment banks.

Stock and Bond Offerings

CHAPTER 6

In this chapter, we will take you through the three basic forms of U.S. public offerings: the IPO, the follow-on equity offering, and the bond offering. Traditionally, the London and other European markets had a variety of local procedures for capital raising but increasingly U.S. forms are becoming standard practice internationally.

Initial Public Offerings

An **initial public offering** (IPO) is the process by which a private company transforms itself into a public company. The company offers, for the first time, shares of its equity (ownership) to the investing public. These shares subsequently trade on a public stock exchange like the London or New York Stock Exchange (NYSE).

The first question you may ask is why a company would want to go public. Many private companies succeed remarkably well as privately owned enterprises. One privately held company, Cargill books more than $60 billion in annual revenue. And until 1999, Wall Street's leading investment bank, Goldman Sachs, was a private company. However, for many large or growing private companies, a day of reckoning comes for the owners when they decide to sell a portion of their ownership in their firm to the public.

The primary reason for going through the rigors of an IPO is to raise cash to fund the growth of a company and to increase the company's ability to make acquisitions using stock. For example, industry observers believe that Goldman Sachs' partners wished to at least have available a publicly traded currency (the stock in the company) with which to acquire other financial services firms.

While obtaining growth capital is the main reason for going public, it is not the only reason. Often, the owners of a company may simply wish to cash out either partially or entirely by selling their ownership in the firm in the offering. Thus, the owners will sell shares in the IPO and get cash for their equity in the firm. Or, sometimes a company's CEO may own a majority or all of the equity, and will offer a few shares in an IPO in order to diversify his/her net worth or to gain some liquidity. To return to the example of Goldman Sachs, some felt that another driving force behind the partners' decision to go public was the feeling that financial markets were at their peak, and that they could get a good price for their equity in their firm. It should be noted that going public is not a slam dunk. Firms

Visit **Vault Europe's Finance Career Channel** at **www.Vault.com/Europe** for insider firm profiles, employee surveys of banking profesionals in Europe, job listings, expert finance career advice, insider salary information and more.

V\ULT CAREER LIBRARY   39

that are too small, too stagnant or have poor growth prospects will — in general — fail to find an investment bank (or at least a top-tier investment bank, known as a "**bulge bracket**" firm) willing to underwrite their IPOs.

From an investment banking perspective, the IPO process consists of these three major phases: hiring the mangers, due diligence, and marketing.

Hiring the managers. The first step for a company wishing to go public is to hire managers for its offering. This choosing of an investment bank is often referred to as a "**beauty contest**." Typically, this process involves meeting with and interviewing investment bankers from different firms, discussing the firm's reasons for going public, and ultimately nailing down a valuation. In making a valuation, I-bankers, through a mix of art and science, pitch to the company wishing to go public what they believe the firm is worth, and therefore how much stock it can realistically sell. Perhaps understandably, companies often choose the bank that predict the highest valuation during this beauty contest phase instead of the best-qualified manager. Almost all IPO candidates select two or more investment banks to manage the IPO process. The primary manager is known as the "**lead manager**,"while additional banks are known as "**co-managers**."

Due diligence and drafting. Once managers are selected, the second phase of the IPO process begins. For investment bankers on the deal, this phase involves understanding the company's business as well as possible scenarios (called **due diligence**), and then filing the legal documents as required by the regulatory authorities. In the U.S., the SEC legal form used by a company issuing new public securities is called the S-1 (or **prospectus**) and requires quite a bit of effort to draft. Lawyers, accountants, I-bankers, and of course company management must all toil for countless hours to complete the S-1 in a timely manner. The final step of filing the completed S-1 usually culminates at "**the printer**" (see sidebar in Chapter 8).

Marketing. The third phase of an IPO is the marketing phase. Once the SEC has approved the prospectus, the company embarks on a **roadshow** to sell the deal. A roadshow involves flying the company's management coast to coast (and often to Europe) to visit institutional investors potentially interested in buying shares in the offering. Typical roadshows last from two to three weeks, and involve meeting literally hundreds of investors, who listen to the company's canned PowerPoint presentation, and then ask scrutinizing questions. Insiders say money managers decide whether or not to invest thousands of dollars in a company within just a few minutes into a presentation.

The marketing phase ends abruptly with the placement and final "pricing" of the stock, which results in a new security trading in the market. Investment banks earn fees by taking a percentage commision (called the "**underwriting discount**," usually around 8 percent for an IPO) on the proceeds of the offering. Successful IPOs will trade up on their first day (increase in share price). Young public companies that miss their numbers are dealt with harshly by institutional investors, who not only sell the stock, causing it to drop precipitously, but also quickly lose confidence in the management team.

Follow-on Offerings of Stock

A company that is already publicly traded will sometimes sell stock to the public again. This type of offering is called a **follow-on offering**, or a secondary offering. One reason for a follow-on offering is the same as a major reason for the initial offering: a company may be growing rapidly, either by making acquisitions or by internal growth, and may simply require additional capital.

Another reason that a company would issue a follow-on offering is similar to the cashing out scenario in the IPO. In a secondary offering, a large existing shareholder (usually the largest shareholder, say, the CEO or founder) may wish to sell a large block of stock in one fell swoop. The reason for this is that this must be done through an additional offering (rather than through a simple sale on the stock market through a broker), is that a company may have shareholders with "unregistered" stock who wish to sell large blocks of their shares. In the U.S., by SEC decree, all stock must first be registered by filing an S-1 or similar document before it can trade on a public stock exchange. Thus, pre-IPO shareholders who do not sell shares in the initial offering hold what is called unregistered stock, and are restricted from selling large blocks unless the company registers them. (The equity owners who hold the shares sold in an offering, whether it be an IPO or a follow-on, are called the selling shareholders.)

Visit **Vault Europe's Finance Career Channel** at **www.Vault.com/Europe** for insider firm profiles, employee surveys of banking profesionals in Europe, job listings, expert finance career advice, insider salary information and more.

VAULT CAREER LIBRARY   41

An Example of a Follow-on Offering:
"New" and "Old" Shares

There are two types of shares that are sold in secondary offerings. When a company requires additional growth capital, it sells "new" shares to the public. When an existing shareholder wishes to sell a huge block of stock, "old" shares are sold to the public. Follow-on offerings often include both types of shares.

Let's look at an example. Suppose Acme Company wished to raise £100 million to fund certain growth prospects. Suppose that at the same time, its biggest shareholder, a venture capital firm, was looking to "cash out," or sell its stock.

Assume the firm already had 100 million shares of stock trading in the market. Let's also say that Acme's stock price traded most recently at £10 per share. The current market value of the firm's equity is:

£10 x 100,000,000 shares = £1,000,000,000 (£1 billion)

Say XYZ Venture Capitalists owned 10 million shares (comprising 10 percent of the firm's equity). They want to sell all of their equity in the firm, or the entire 10 million shares. And to raise £100 million of new capital, Acme would have to sell 10 million additional (or new) shares of stock to the public. These shares would be newly created during the offering process. In fact, the prospectus for the follow-on legally "registers" the stock with the Financial Services Authority (FSA), the financial services industry regulator which is referred to as the UK Listing Authority (UKLA) when acting as the authority for listing shares on a stock exchange, thus authorising the sale of stock to investors.

The total size of the deal would thus need to be 20 million shares, 10 million of which are "new" and 10 million of which are coming from the selling shareholders, the VC firm. Interestingly, because of the additional shares and what is called "dilution of earnings" or "dilution of EPS," stock prices typically trade down upon a follow-on offering announcement. (Of course, this only happens if the stock to be issued in the deal is "new" stock.)

After this secondary offering is completed, Acme would have 110 million shares outstanding, and its market value would be £1.1 billion if the stock remains at £10 per share. And, the shares sold by XYZ Venture Capitalists will now be in the hands of new investors in the form of freely tradable securities.

Market reaction. What happens when a company announces a secondary offering indicates the market's tolerance for additional equity. Because more shares of stock "dilute" the old shareholders, and "dumps" shares of stock for sale on the market, the stock price usually drops on the announcement of a follow-on offering. **Dilution** occurs because earnings per share (EPS) in the future will decline, simply based on the fact that more shares will exist post-deal. And since EPS drives stock prices, the share price generally drops.

The process. The follow-on offering process differs little from that of an IPO, and actually is far less complicated. Since underwriters have already represented the company in an IPO, a company often chooses the same managers, thus making the hiring the manager or beauty contest phase much simpler. Also, no real valuation work is required (the market now values the firm's stock), a prospectus has already been written, and a roadshow presentation already prepared. Modifications to the prospectus and the roadshow demand the most time in a follow-on offering, but still can usually be completed with a fraction of the effort required for an initial offering.

Bond Offerings

When a company requires capital, it sometimes chooses to issue **public debt** instead of equity. Almost always, however, a firm undergoing a public bond deal will already have stock trading in the market. (It is relatively rare for a private company to issue bonds before its IPO.)

The reasons for issuing bonds rather than stock are various. Perhaps the stock price of the issuer is down, and thus a bond issue is a better alternative. Or perhaps the firm does not wish to dilute its existing shareholders by issuing more equity. Or perhaps a company is quite profitable and wants the tax deduction from paying bond interest, while issuing stock offers no tax deduction. These are all valid reasons for issuing bonds rather than equity. Sometimes in down markets, investor appetite for public offerings dwindles to the point where an equity deal just could not get done (investors would not buy the issue).

The bond offering process resembles the IPO process. The primary difference lies in: (1) the focus of the prospectus (a prospectus for a bond offering will emphasize the company's stability and steady cash flow, whereas a stock prospectus will usually play up the company's growth and expansion opportunities), and (2) the importance of the bond's credit rating (the company will want to obtain a favorable credit rating from a debt rating agency like S&P or Moody's, with the help of the "credit department" of the investment

Visit **Vault Europe's Finance Career Channel** at **www.Vault.com/Europe** for insider firm profiles, employee surveys of banking profesionals in Europe, job listings, expert finance career advice, insider salary information and more.

VAULT   CAREER
LIBRARY   43

bank issuing the bond; the bank's credit department will negotiate with the rating agencies to obtain the best possible rating). As covered in Chapter 5, the better the credit rating — and therefore, the safer the bonds — the lower the interest rate the company must pay on the bonds to entice investors to buy the issue. Clearly, a firm issuing debt will want to have the highest possible bond rating, and hence pay a lower interest rate (or yield).

As with stock offerings, investment banks earn underwriting fees on bond offerings in the form of an underwriting discount on the proceeds of the offering. The percentage fee for bond underwriting tends to be lower than for stock underwriting. For more detail on your role as an investment banker in stock and bond offerings, see Chapter 8.

Mergers and Aquisitions, Private Placements, and Reorganizations

CHAPTER 7

Mergers & Acquisitions

In the 1980s, hostile takeovers and LBO acquisitions were all the rage. Companies sought to acquire others through aggressive stock purchases and cared little about the target company's concerns. The 1990s were the decade of friendly mergers, dominated by a few sectors of the economy. Mergers in the telecommunications, financial services, and technology industries were commanding headlines, as these sectors went through dramatic change, both regulatory and financial. But giant mergers were occurring in virtually every industry (witness one of the biggest of them all, the merger between Exxon and Mobil). Except for short periods of market volatility, **M&A** (mergers and acquisitions) business was brisk in the 1990s, as demands to go global, to keep pace with the competition, and to expand earnings by any possible means were foremost in the minds of CEOs.

At the beginning of the millennium, however, M&A activity slowed, hitting bottom in 2002 when the value of deals crashed by 40 percent. But activity began to revive in 2003: in 2005, worldwide volume rose by 38 per cent versus 2004; and in the first quarter of 2006 it surged 45 percent.

When a public company acquires another public company, the target company's stock often rises while the acquiring company's stock often declines. Why? One must realize that existing shareholders must be convinced to sell their stock. Few shareholders are willing to sell their stock to an acquirer without first being paid a premium on the current stock price. In addition, shareholders must also capture a takeover premium to relinquish control over the stock. The large shareholders of the target company typically demand such an extraction. (Usually once a takeover is announced, the "arbs" or arbitragers, buy up shares on the open market and drive up the share price to near the proposed takeover price.)

M&A transactions can be roughly divided into either mergers or acquisitions. These terms are often used interchangeably in the press, and the actual legal difference between the two involves arcana of accounting procedures, but we can still draw a rough difference between the two.

Visit **Vault Europe's Finance Career Channel** at www.Vault.com/Europe for insider firm profiles, employee surveys of banking profesionals in Europe, job listings, expert finance career advice, insider salary information and more.

VAULT CAREER LIBRARY 45

Acquisition — When a larger company takes over another (smaller firm) and clearly becomes the new owner, the purchase is typically called an acquisition on Wall Street. Typically, the target company ceases to exist post-transaction (from a legal corporation point of view) and the acquiring corporation swallows the business. The stock of the acquiring company continues to be traded.

Merger — A merger occurs when two companies, often roughly of the same size, combine to create a new company. Such a situation is often called a "merger of equals." Both companies' stocks are tendered (or given up), and new company stock is issued in its place. For example, both Chrysler and Daimler-Benz ceased to exist when their firms merged, and a new combined company, DaimlerChrysler was created.

M&A advisory services

For an I-bank, M&A advising is highly profitable, and there are many possibilities for types of transactions. Perhaps a small private company's owner/manager wishes to sell out for cash and retire. Or perhaps a big public firm aims to buy a competitor through a stock swap. Whatever the case, M&A advisors come directly from the corporate finance departments of investment banks. Unlike public offerings, merger transactions do not directly involve salespeople, traders or research analysts, although research analysts in particular can play an important role in "blessing" the merger. In particular, M&A advisory falls onto the laps of M&A specialists and fits into one of either two buckets: seller representation or buyer representation (also called **target representation** and **acquirer representation**).

Representing the target

An I-bank that represents a potential seller has a much greater likelihood of completing a transaction (and therefore being paid) than an I-bank that represents a potential acquirer. Also known as sell-side work, this type of advisory assignment is generated by a company that approaches an investment bank (also an investment bank may also make the initial approach and "pitch" the idea of the company being sold or merged) and asks the bank to find a buyer of either the entire company or a division. Often, sell-side representation comes when a company asks an investment bank to help it sell a division, plant or subsidiary operation.

Buyout Firms and LBOs

Buyout firms, which are also called financial sponsors, acquire companies by borrowing substantial cash. These buyout firms (also called LBO firms) implement a management team they trust, improve sales and profits, and ultimately seek an exit strategy (usually a sale or IPO) for their investment within a few years. These firms are driven to achieve a high return on investment (ROI), and focus their efforts toward streamlining the acquired business and preparing the company for a future IPO or sale. It is quite common that a buyout firm will be the selling shareholder in an IPO or follow-on offering.

Generally speaking, the work involved in finding a buyer includes writing a Selling Memorandum and then contacting potential strategic or financial buyers of the client. If the client hopes to sell a semiconductor plant, for instance, the I-bankers will contact firms in that industry, as well as buyout firms that focus on purchasing technology or high-tech manufacturing operations.

Representing the acquirer

In advising sellers, the I-bank's work is complete once another party purchases the business up for sale, i.e., once another party buys your client's company or division or assets. Buy-side work is an entirely different animal. The advisory work itself is straightforward: the investment bank contacts the firm their client wishes to purchase, attempts to structure a palatable offer for all parties, and makes the deal a reality. (Again, the initial contact may be from the acquiring company. Or the investment bank may "pitch" the idea of an acquisition of Company X to the acquiring company.) However, most of these proposals do not work out; few firms or owners are willing to readily sell their business. And because the I-banks primarily collect fees based on completed transactions, their work often goes unpaid.

Consequently, when advising clients looking to buy a business, an I-bank's work often drags on for months. Often a firm will pay a non-refundable retainer fee to hire a bank and say, "Find us a target company to buy." These acquisition searches can last for months and produce nothing except associate and analyst fatigue as they repeatedly build merger models and pull all-nighters. Deals that do get done, though, are a boon for the I-bank representing the buyer because of their enormous profitability. Typical fees depend on the size of the deal, but generally fall in the 1 percent range. For a $100 million deal, an investment bank takes home $1 million. Not bad for a few months' work.

Visit Vault Europe's Finance Career Channel at www.Vault.com/Europe for insider firm profiles, employee surveys of banking profesionals in Europe, job listings, expert finance career advice, insider salary information and more.

VAULT CAREER
LIBRARY   47

Private Placements

A **private placement**, which involves the selling of debt or equity to private investors, resembles both a public offering and a merger. A private placement differs little from a public offering aside from the fact that a private placement involves a firm selling stock or equity to private investors rather than to public investors. Also, a typical private placement deal is smaller than a public transaction. Despite these differences, the primary reason for a private placement — to raise capital — is fundamentally the same as a public offering.

Why private placements?

As mentioned previously, firms wishing to raise capital often discover that they are unable to go public for a number of reasons. The company may not be big enough; the markets may not have an appetite for IPOs, the company may be too young or not ready to be a public company, or the company may simply prefer not to have its stock be publicly traded. Such firms with solidly growing businesses make excellent private placement candidates. Often, firms wishing to go public may be advised by investment bankers to first do a private placement, as they need to gain critical mass or size to justify an IPO.

Private placements, then, are usually the province of smaller companies aiming ultimately to go public. The process of raising private equity or debt changes only slightly from a public deal. One difference is that private placements do not involve a roadshow and in the U.S., the securities do not have to be registered with the SEC. In place of the prospectus, I-banks draft a detailed **Private Placement Memorandum** (PPM for short) which divulges information similar to a prospectus. Instead of a roadshow, companies looking to sell private stock or debt will host potential investors as interest arises, and give presentations detailing how they will be the greatest thing since sliced bread.

Often, one firm will be the sole or lead investor in a private placement. In other words, if a company sells stock through a private placement, often only one venture capital firm or institution will buy most or all of the stock offered. Conversely, in an IPO, shares of stock fall into the hands of literally thousands of buyers immediately after the deal is completed.

The I-bank's role in private placements

The investment banker's work involved in a private placement is quite similar to sell-side M&A representation. The bankers attempt to find a buyer by writing the PPM and then contacting potential strategic or financial buyers of the client.

In the case of private placements, however, financial buyers are typically venture capitalists rather than buyout firms, which is an important distinction. A VC firm invests in less than 50 percent of a company's equity, whereas a buyout firm purchases greater than 50 percent and often nearly 100 percent of a company's equity, thereby gaining control of the firm. Note that the same difference applies to private placements on the sell-side. A sale occurs when a firm sells greater than 50 percent of its equity (giving up control), but a private placement occurs usually when less than 50 percent of its equity is sold. Note that in private placements, the company typically offers convertible preferred stock, rather than common stock.

Because private placements involve selling equity and debt to a single buyer, the investor and the seller (the company) typically negotiate the terms of the deal. Investment bankers function as negotiators for the company, helping to convince the investor of the value of the firm.

Fees involved in private placements work like those in public offerings. Usually they are a fixed percentage of the size of the transaction. (Of course, the fees depend on whether a deal is consummated or not.) A common private placement fee is 5 to 8 percent of the size of the equity/ debt sold.

Financial Restructurings

When a company cannot pay its cash obligations — for example, when it cannot meet its bond payments or its payments to other creditors (such as vendors) — it usually must file for bankruptcy court protection from creditors. In this situation, a company can, of course, choose to simply shut down operations and walk away. On the other hand, it can also **restructure** and remain in business.

What does it mean to restructure? The process can be thought of as two-fold: financial restructuring and organizational restructuring. Restructuring from a financial viewpoint involves renegotiating payment terms on debt obligations, issuing new debt, and restructuring payables to vendors. Bankers provide guidance to the restructuring firm by recommending the sale of assets, the issuing of special securities such as convertible stock and bonds, or even working with M&A bankers to sell the company entirely.

From an organizational viewpoint, a restructuring can involve a change in management, strategy and focus. I-bankers with expertise in "reorgs" can facilitate and ease the transition from bankruptcy to viability.

isit **Vault Europe's Finance Career Channel** at **www.Vault.com/Europe** for insider firm
rofiles, employee surveys of banking profesionals in Europe, job listings, expert finance
areer advice, insider salary information and more.

VAULT CAREER LIBRARY

49

Fees in restructuring work

Typical investment banking fees in a restructuring depend on what new securities are issued post-bankruptcy and whether the company is sold, but usually includes a retainer fee paid upfront to the investment bank. When a bank represents a bankrupt company, the brunt of the work is focused on analyzing and recommending financing alternatives. Thus, the fee structure resembles that of a private placement. How does the work differ from that of a private placement? I-bankers not only work in securing financing, but may assist in building projections for the client (which serve to illustrate to potential financiers what the firm's prospects may be), in renegotiating credit terms with lenders working with the company's lawyers to navigate through the bankruptcy court process, and in helping to re-establish the business as a going concern.

Because a firm in bankruptcy already has substantial cash flow problems, investment banks often charge minimal monthly retainers, hoping to cash in on the spread from issuing new securities or selling the company. Like other offerings, this can be a highly lucrative and steady business.

ON THE JOB

Corporate Finance

CHAPTER 8

Stuffy bankers?

The stereotype of the **corporate finance** department is stuffy, arrogant (white and male) MBAs who frequent golf courses and talk on cell-phones nonstop. While this is increasingly less true, corporate finance remains the most elite department in the typical investment bank. The atmosphere in corporate finance is, unlike that in sales and trading, often quiet and reserved. Junior bankers sit separated by cubicles, quietly crunching numbers.

Depending on the firm, corporate finance can also be a tough place to work, with unforgiving bankers and expectations through the roof. Although decreasing, stories of analyst abuse abound, and some bankers come down hard on new analysts to scare and intimidate them. The lifestyle for corporate finance professionals can be a killer. In fact, many corporate finance workers find that they literally dedicate their lives to the job. Social life suffers, free time disappears, and stress multiplies. It is not uncommon to find analysts and associates wearing rumpled pants and wrinkled shirts, exhibiting the wear and tear of all-nighters. Fortunately, these long hours pay remarkable dividends in the form of six-figure salaries and huge year-end bonuses.

Personality-wise, bankers tend to be highly intelligent, motivated, and not lacking in confidence. Money is important to the bankers, and many anticipate working for just a few years to earn as much as possible, before finding less demanding work. Analysts and associates tend also to be ambitious, intelligent and pedigreed. If you happen to be going into an analyst or associate position, make sure to check your ego at the door but don't be afraid to ask penetrating questions about deals and what is required of you.

The deal team

Investment bankers generally work in **deal teams** which, depending on the size of a deal, vary somewhat in makeup. In this chapter we will provide an overview of the roles and lifestyles of the positions in corporate finance, from analyst to managing director. (Often, a person in corporate finance is generally called an I-banker.) Because the titles and roles really do not differ significantly between underwriting to M&A, we have included both in this explanation. In fact, at most smaller firms, underwriting and transaction advisory are not separated, and bankers typically pitch whatever business they can scout out within their industry sector.

it **Vault Europe's Finance Career Channel** at **www.Vault.com/Europe** for insider firm files, employee surveys of banking profesionals in Europe, job listings, expert finance eer advice, insider salary information and more.

V/\ULT CAREER LIBRARY 53

The Players

Analysts

Analysts are the grunts of the corporate finance world. They often toil endlessly with little thanks, little pay (when figured on an hourly basis), and barely enough free time to sleep four hours a night. Typically hired directly out of top undergraduate universities, this crop of bright, highly motivated kids does the financial modeling and basic entry-level duties associated with any corporate finance deal.

Modeling every night until 2 a.m. and not having much of a social life proves to be unbearable for many an analyst and after two years many analysts leave the industry. Unfortunately, many bankers recognize the transient nature of analysts, and work them hard to get the most out of them they can. The unfortunate analyst that screws up or talks back too much may never get quality work, spending his days bored until 11 p.m. waiting for work to come, stressing even more than the busy analyst. These are the analysts that do not get called to work on live transactions, and do menial work or just put together pitchbooks all the time.

Salaries for first-year analysts in the City at a major investment bank begin around £30,000 to £40,000 per year, with an annual bonus of perhaps £15,000. While this seems to be a lot for a 22-year -old with just an undergrad degree, it's not a great deal if you consider per-hour compensation. At most firms, analysts also get dinner every night for free if they work late, and have little time to spend their income, often meaning fat current and deposit accounts and ample means to fund business school of law school down the road. While the salary does not improve much for second-year analysts, the bonus can double for those second years who demonstrate high performance. At this level, bonuses depend mostly on an analyst's contribution, attitude, and work ethic, as opposed to the volume of business generated by the bankers with whom he or she works.

Associates

Much like analysts, associates hit the grindstone hard. Working 80- to 100-hour weeks, associates stress over pitchbooks and models all night, become experts with financial modeling on Excel, and sometimes shake their heads wondering what the point is. Unlike analysts, however, associates more quickly become involved with clients and, most importantly, are not at the foot of the ladder. Associates quickly learn to delegate and hand-off menial modeling work and research projects to analysts. However, treatment from vice presidents and managing directors doesn't necessarily improve for associates versus analysts, as bankers sometimes care more about the work getting done, and not about the guy or gal working away all night to complete it.

Usually hailing directly from top business schools (sometimes law schools or other grad schools), associates often possess only a summer's worth of experience in corporate finance, so they must start almost from the beginning. Associates who worked as analysts before grad school have a little more experience under their belts. The overall level of business awareness and knowledge a bright MBA has, however, makes a tremendous difference, and associates quickly earn the luxury of more complicated work, client contact, and bigger bonuses.

Associates are at least much better paid than analysts. They generally start off at a salary of £40,000 to £50,000, and usually bonuses hit £20,000 and up in the first six months. (At most firms, associates start in August and get their first prorated bonus in January.) Newly minted MBAs cash in on signing bonuses and sometimes forgivable loans as well. These can be worth maybe another £15,000 to £20,000, depending on the firm, providing total first-year compensation of perhaps as much as £100,000 at top firms. Associates beyond their first year begin to rake it in, earning £120,000 to £200,000 and up per year, depending on the firm's profitability and other factors.

Vice Presidents

Upon attaining the position of vice president (at most firms, after four or five years as associates), those in corporate finance enter the realm of real bankers. The lifestyle becomes more manageable once the associate moves up to VP. On the plus side, weekends sometimes free up, all-nighters drop off, and the general level of responsibility increases — VPs are the ones telling associates and analysts to stay late on Friday nights. In the office, VPs manage the financial modeling/pitchbook production process in the office. On the negative side, the wear and tear of traveling that accompanies VP-level banker responsibilities can be difficult. As a VP, one begins to handle client relationships, and thus spends much more time on the road than analysts or associates. You can look forward to being on the road at least two to four days per week, usually visiting clients and potential clients. Don't forget about closing dinners (to celebrate completed deals), industry conferences (to drum up potential business and build a solid network within their industry), and, of course, roadshows. VPs are perfect candidates to baby-sit company management on roadshows.

sit **Vault Europe's Finance Career Channel** at **www.Vault.com/Europe** for insider firm ofiles, employee surveys of banking profesionals in Europe, job listings, expert finance reer advice, insider salary information and more.

VAULT CAREER LIBRARY 55

Directors/Managing Directors

Directors and managing directors (MDs) are the major players in corporate finance. Typically, MDs set their own hours, deal with clients at the highest level, and disappear whenever a drafting session takes place, leaving this grueling work to others. (We will examine these drafting sessions in depth later.) MDs mostly develop and cultivate relationships with various companies in order to generate corporate finance business for the firm. MDs typically focus on one industry, develop relationships among management teams of companies in the industry and visit these companies on a regular basis. These visits are aptly called sales calls.

Pay scales

The formula for paying bankers varies dramatically from firm to firm. Some adhere to rigid formulas based on how much business a banker brought in, while others pay based on a subjective allocation of corporate finance profits. No matter how compensation is structured, however, when business is slow, bonuses taper off rapidly. For most bankers, typical salaries may range from £60,000 to £120,000 per year, but bonuses can be significantly greater. Total packages for VPs in the City may hit over the £250,000 level in the first year — and pay can skyrocket from there.

Top bankers at the MD level might be pulling in bonuses of up to £500,000 or more a year, but slow markets (and hence slow business) can cut that number dramatically. It is important to realize that for the most part, MDs act as relationship managers, and are essentially paid on commission. For top performers, compensation can be almost inconceivable.

The Role of the Players

What do corp fin professionals actually do on a day-to-day basis to underwrite an offering? The process, though not simple, can easily be broken up into the same three phases that we described previously. We will illustrate the role of the bankers by walking through the IPO process in more detail. Note that other types of stock or debt offerings closely mirror the IPO process.

Hiring the managers

This phase in the process can vary in length substantially, lasting for many months or just a few short weeks. The length of the hiring phase depends on how many I-banks the company wishes to meet, when they want to go public, and how market conditions fare. Remember that two or more investment banks are usually tapped to manage a single equity or debt deal, complicating the hiring decisions that companies face.

MDs and sales calls

Often when a large IPO candidate is preparing for an offering, word gets out that the company is looking to go public. MDs all over the City and Wall Street scramble to create pitchbooks (see sidebar on next page) and set up meetings called "**pitches**" in order to convince the company to hire them as the lead manager. I-bankers who have previously established a good relationship with the company have a distinct advantage. What is surprising to many people unfamiliar with I-banking is that MDs are essentially traveling salespeople who pay visits to the CEOs and CFOs of companies, with the goal of building investment banking relationships.

Typically, MDs meet informally with the company several times. In an initial meeting with a firm's management, the MD will have an analyst and an associate put together a general pitchbook, which is left with the company to illustrate the I-bank's capabilities.

Once an MD knows a company plans to go public, he or she will first discuss the IPO with the company's top management and gather data regarding past financial performance and future expected results. This data, farmed out to a VP or associate and crucial to the valuation, is then used in the preparation of the pitchbook.

Visit Vault Europe's Finance Career Channel at www.Vault.com/Europe for insider firm profiles, employee surveys of banking profesionals in Europe, job listings, expert finance career advice, insider salary information and more.

VAULT CAREER LIBRARY

57

A Word About Pitchbooks

Pitchbooks come in two flavors: the general pitchbook and the deal-specific pitchbook. Bankers use the general pitchbook to guide their introductions and presentations during sales calls. These pitchbooks contain general information and include a wide variety of selling points bankers make to potential clients. Usually, general pitchbooks include an overview of the I-bank and detail its specific capabilities in research, corporate finance, sales and trading.

The second flavor of pitchbooks is the deal-specific pitch. While a general pitchbook does not differ much from deal to deal, bankers prepare offering pitchbooks specifically for the transactions (for example, an IPO or proposed sale of the company) they are proposing to a company's top managers. Deal-specific pitchbooks are highly customized and usually require at least one analyst or associate all-nighter to put together (although MDs, VPs, associates, and analysts all work closely together to create the book). The most difficult aspect to creating this type of pitchbook is the financial modeling involved. In an IPO pitchbook, valuations, comparable company analyses, and industry analyses are but a few of the many specific topics covered in detail.

Apart from the numbers, these pitchbooks also include the bank's customized selling points. The most common of these include:

- The bank's reputation, which can lend the offering an aura of respectability

- The performance of other IPOs or similar offerings managed by the bank

- The prominence of a bank's research analyst in the industry, which can tacitly guarantee that the new public stock will receive favorable coverage by a listened-to stock expert

- The bank's expertise as an underwriter in the industry, including its ranking in the "league tables" (rankings of investment banks based on their volume of offerings handled in a given category)

Pitchbook preparation

After substantial effort and probably a few all-nighters on the part of analysts and associates, the deal-specific pitchbook is complete. The most important piece of information in this kind of pitchbook is the valuation of the company going public. Prior to its initial public offering, a company has no public equity and therefore no clear market value of common stock. So, the investment bankers, through a mix of financial and industry expertise, including analysis of comparable public companies, develop a suitable offering size range and hence a marketable valuation range for the company. Of course, the higher the valuation, the happier the potential client. At the same time, though, I-bankers must not be too aggressive in their valuation — if the market does not support the valuation and the IPO fails, the bank loses credibility.

The pitch

While analysts and associates are the members of the **deal team** who spend the most time working on the pitchbook, the MD is the one who actually visits the company with the books under his or her arm to make the pitch, perhaps with a VP. The pitchbook serves as a guide for the presentation (led by the MD) to the company. This presentation generally concludes with the valuation. Companies invite many I-banks to present their pitches at separate meetings. These multiple rounds of presentations comprise what is often called the beauty contest or beauty pageant.

The pitch comes from the managing director in charge of the deal. The MD's supporting cast typically consists of a VP from corporate finance, as well as the research analyst who will cover the company's stock once the IPO is complete. For especially important pitches, an I-bank will send other top representatives from either its corporate finance, research or syndicate departments. (We will cover the syndicate and research departments later.) Some companies opt to have their board of directors sit in on the pitch — the MD might face the added pressure of tough questions from the board during the presentation.

Selecting the managers

After a company has seen all of the pitches in a beauty contest, it selects one firm as the lead manager, while some of the other firms are chosen as the co-managers. The number of firms chosen to manage a deal runs the gamut. Sometimes a firm will sole manage a deal, and sometimes, especially on large global deals, four to six firms might be selected as managers. An average-sized offering will generally have three to four managers underwriting the offering — one lead manager and two or three co-managers.

sit **Vault Europe's Finance Career Channel** at www.Vault.com/Europe for insider firm ofiles, employee surveys of banking profesionals in Europe, job listings, expert finance reer advice, insider salary information and more.

VAULT CAREER LIBRARY 59

Due diligence and drafting

Organizational meeting

Once the I-bank has been selected as a manager in the IPO, the next step is an organizational meeting at the company's headquarters. All parties in the working group involved in the deal meet for the first time, shake hands and get down to business. The attendees and their roles are summarized in the table below.

Group	Typical Participants
The Company	Management, namely the CEO and CFO, division heads, and heads of major departments or lines of business.
The Company's lawyers	Partner plus one associate.
The Company's accountants	Partner, plus one or two associates.
The lead manager	I-banking team, with up to four corporate finance professionals. A research analyst may come for due diligence meetings.
The co-manager(s), or I-bank(s) selected behind the lead	I-banking team with typically two or three members instead of four.
Underwriters' counsel, or the lawyers representing the managers	Partner plus one associate.

At the initial organizational meeting, the MD from the lead manager guides and moderates the meeting. Details discussed at the meeting include the exact size of the offering, the timetable for completing the deal, and other concerns the group may have. Usually a two- or three-month schedule is established as a beacon toward the completion of the offering. A sheet is distributed so all parties can list home, office, and cell phone numbers. Often, the organizational meeting wraps up in an hour or two and leads directly to due diligence.

Due diligence

Due diligence involves studying the company going public in as much detail as possible. Much of this process involves interviewing senior management at the firm. Due diligence usually entails a plant tour (if relevant), and explanations of the company's business, how the company operates, how management plans to grow the company, and how the company will perform over the next few quarters.

As with the organizational meeting, the moderator and lead questioner throughout the due diligence sessions is the senior banker in attendance from the lead manager. Research analysts from the I-banks attend the due diligence meetings during the IPO process in order to probe the business, ask tough questions and generally better understand how to project the company's financials. While bankers tend to focus on the relevant operational, financial, and strategic issues at the firm, lawyers involved in the deal explore mostly legal issues, such as pending litigation.

Drafting the prospectus

Once due diligence wraps up, the IPO process moves quickly into the drafting stage. Drafting refers to the process by which the working group writes the prospectus. This prospectus provides detailed financial information and is the document used to market the offering to potential investors.

Generally, the client company's lawyers ("issuer's counsel") compile the first draft of the prospectus, but thereafter the drafting process includes the entire working group. Unfortunately, writing by committee means a multitude of style clashes, disagreements, and tangential discussions, but the end result usually is a prospectus that most team members can live with. On average, the drafting stage takes anywhere from four to seven drafting sessions, spread over a six- to 10-week period. Initially, all of the top corp fin representatives from each of the managers attends, but these meetings thin out to fewer and fewer members as they continue. The lead manager will always have at least a VP to represent the firm, but co-managers often settle on VPs, associates, and sometimes even analysts to represent their firms.

Drafting sessions are initially exciting to attend as an analyst or associate, as they offer client exposure, learning about a business, and getting out of the office. However, these sessions can quickly grow tiring and annoying. Final drafting sessions at the printer can mean more all-nighters, as the group scrambles to finish the prospectus on time.

Visit **Vault Europe's Finance Career Channel** at www.Vault.com/Europe for insider firm profiles, employee surveys of banking profesionals in Europe, job listings, expert finance career advice, insider salary information and more.

V/\ULT CAREER LIBRARY 61

Going to the Printer

When a prospectus is near completion, lawyers, bankers and the company's senior management all go to the printer, which, as one insider says, is "sort of like going to a country club prison." These 24-hour financial printers, where prospectuses are actually printed, are equipped with showers, all the food you can eat, and other amenities to accommodate locked-in-until-you're-done sessions.

Printers are employed by companies to print and distribute prospectus. A typical Wall Street public deal requires anywhere from 10,000 to 20,000 copies of the preliminary prospectus (called the red herring or red) and 5,000 to 10,000 copies of the final prospectus. Printers receive the final edited version from the working group, literally print the thousands of copies in-house and then mail them to potential investors in a deal. (The list of investors comes from the managers.) In the U.S., printers also file the document electronically with the SEC via the "EDGAR" system. As the last meeting before the prospectus is completed, printer meetings can last anywhere from a day to a week or even more. Why is this significant? Because printers are extraordinarily expensive and companies are eager to move onto the next phase of the deal. This amounts to loads of pressure on the working group to finish the prospectus.

For those in the working group, perfecting the prospectus means wrangling over commas, legal language, and grammar until the document is error-free. Nothing is allowed to interrupt a printer meeting, meaning one or two all-nighters in a row is not unheard of for working groups.

On the plus side, printers stock anything and everything that a person could want to eat or drink. The best restaurants cater to printers, and M&M's always seem to appear on the table just when you want a handful. And food isn't all: Many printers have pool tables and stocked bars for those half-hour breaks at 2:00 a.m. Needless to say, an abundance of coffee and fattening food keeps the group going during late hours.

Marketing

Designing marketing material

When the prospectus is finally ready, and any required regulatory filings have been made, the printer spits out thousands of copies, which are mailed to literally the entire universe of potential institutional investors.

In the meantime, the MD and VP of the lead manager work closely with the CEO and CFO of the company to develop a roadshow presentation, which consists of essentially 20 to 40 slides for use during meetings with investors. Junior team members in corporate finance help edit the roadshow slides and begin working on other marketing documents. For example, associates and analysts develop a summary rehash of the prospectus in a brief "selling memo," which is distributed to the bank's salesforce and contains key selling points for salespeople to use in pitching the offering to clients.

The roadshow (baby sitting)

The actual **roadshow** begins soon after the reds are printed. The preliminary prospectus, called in the U.S. a red herring or red, helps salespeople and investors alike understand the IPO candidate's business, historical financial performance, growth opportunities and risk factors. Using the prospectus and the selling memo as references, the salespeople of the investment banks managing the deal contact the institutional investors they cover and set up roadshow meetings. The syndicate department, the facilitators between the salesperson and corporate finance, finalizes the morass of meetings and communicates the agenda to corporate finance and sales. And, on the roadshow itself, VPs or associates generally escort the company. Despite the seemingly glamorous nature of a roadshow (traveling all over the country in limos and chartered jets with your client, the CEO), the corporate finance professional acts as little more than a babysitter on the roadshow. The most important duties of the junior corporate finance professionals often include making sure luggage gets from point A to point B, ensuring that hotel rooms are booked, and finding the limousine driver at the airport terminal.

After a grueling two to three weeks and hundreds of presentations, the roadshow ends and the group flies home for much needed rest. During the roadshow, sales and syndicate departments compile orders for the company's stock and develop what is called "the book." The book details how investors have responded, how much stock they want (if any), and at what price they are willing to buy into the offering.

Visit **Vault Europe's Finance Career Channel** at www.Vault.com/Europe for insider firm profiles, employee surveys of banking profesionals in Europe, job listings, expert finance career advice, insider salary information and more.

VAULT CAREER LIBRARY 63

Going Public

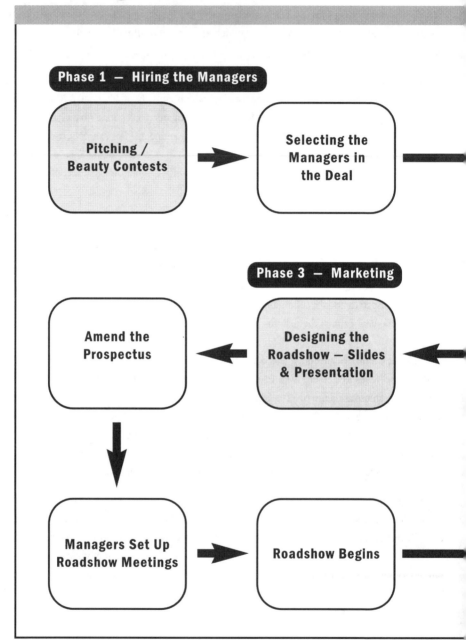

Phase 1 — Hiring the Managers

Pitching / Beauty Contests → Selecting the Managers in the Deal →

Phase 3 — Marketing

Amend the Prospectus ← Designing the Roadshow — Slides & Presentation ←

Managers Set Up Roadshow Meetings → Roadshow Begins

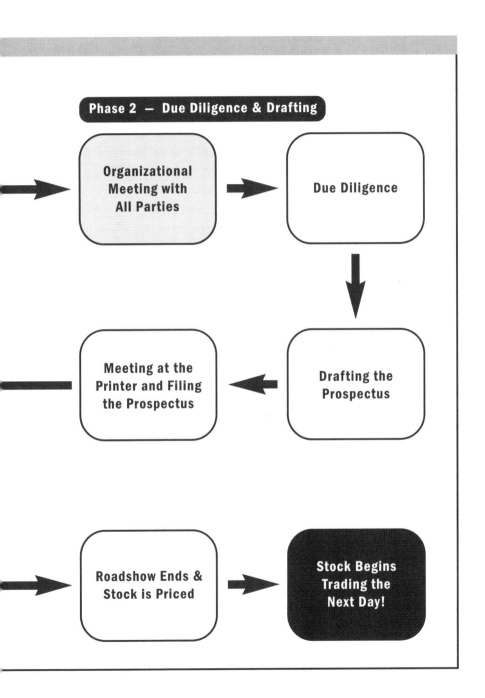

Phase 2 — Due Diligence & Drafting

Organizational Meeting with All Parties

Due Diligence

Meeting at the Printer and Filing the Prospectus

Drafting the Prospectus

Roadshow Ends & Stock is Priced

Stock Begins Trading the Next Day!

Visit **Vault Europe's Finance Career Channel** at **www.Vault.com/Europe** for insider firm profiles, employee surveys of banking profesionals in Europe, job listings, expert finance career advice, insider salary information and more.

VAULT   CAREER LIBRARY   65

The end in sight — pricing the deal

IPO prospectuses list a range of stock prices on the cover (for example, between £16 to £18 per share). This range is preset by the underwriting team before the roadshow and meant to tell investors what the company is worth and hence where it will price. Highly sought-after offerings will price at or even above the top of the range and those in less demand will price at the bottom of the range.

Hot IPOs with tremendous demand end up above the range and often trade up significantly on the first day in the market. The hottest offerings have closed two to three times higher than the initial offering price. Memorable examples in the U.S. stock markets include Apple Computer in the 1980s, Boston Chicken in the mid-90s, and Netscape Communications and a slew of Internet stocks in late 1998 through early 2000. The process of going public is summarized graphically on pages 64-65. More recently, though, hot offerings have seen more modest first-day rises. Google's stock, offered to the public in August 2004, only increased 18 percent on its initial day of trading.

Follow-on public offerings and bond offerings

Bond deals and follow-on offerings are less complex in nature than IPOs for many reasons. The biggest reason is that they have an already agreed-upon and approved prospectus from prior publicly filed documents. The language, content, and style of the prospectus usually stay updated year to year, as the company either files for additional offerings or files its annual report. Also, the fact that the legal hurdles involved in registering a company's securities have already been leaped makes life significantly easier for everyone involved in a follow-on or bond offering.

If a follow-on offering involves the I-banks that handled a company's IPO (and they often do), the MDs that worked on the deal are already familiar with the company. They may not even have to develop a pitchbook to formally pitch the follow-on if the relationship is sound. Because the banking relationship is usually between individual bankers and individual executives at client companies, bankers can often take clients with them if they switch banks.

Because of their relative simplicity, follow-ons and bond deals quickly jump from the manager-choosing phase to the due diligence and drafting phase, which also progresses more quickly than it would for an IPO. The roadshow proceeds as before, with the company and a corp fin VP or associate accompanying management to ensure that the logistics work out.

The Typical Week in Corporate Finance

One of the most common questions an interviewee asks is "What is the typical day for an investment banker like?" Truth be told, days spent in investment banking often vary widely, depending on what aspect of a deal you might be working on. But because deals are similar, you might be able to conjure up a typical week in the life of an analyst, associate, vice president, or managing director in corporate finance. We'll start with analysts.

Analysts

For I-banking analysts, it's all about the computer screen. Analysts, especially those in their first year, spend countless hours staring at their computer monitors and working until midnight or all night. Building models, creating "comps," (see sidebar) and editing pitchbooks fills the majority of their time. Many analysts do nothing but put together pitchbooks, and never see the light of day. Hard working and talented analysts, however, tend to find their way out of the office and become involved in meetings related to live transactions.

A typical week for an analyst might involve the following:

Monday

Up at 7:30 a.m. Monday morning, the analyst makes it into the office by 9. Mornings often move at a snail's pace, so the analyst builds a set of comparable company analysis (a.k.a. comps, see sidebar) and then updates the latest league table data, which track how many deals I-banks have completed. Lunch is a leisurely forty-five minutes spent with other analysts at a deli a few blocks away. The afternoon includes a conference call with a company considering an IPO, and at 5, a meeting with a VP who drops a big model on the analyst's lap. Dinner is delivered at 8 and paid for by the firm, but this is no great joy — it is going to be a late night because of the model. At midnight, the analyst has reached a stopping point and calls a car service to give him a free ride home.

Tuesday

The next day is similar, but the analyst spends all day working on a pitchbook for a meeting on Wednesday that a banker has set up. Of course, the banker waited until the day before the meeting to tell the analyst about it. After working all night and into the morning, including submitting numerous changes to the 24-hour word processing department, the

Visit **Vault Europe's Finance Career Channel** at **www.Vault.com/Europe** for insider firm profiles, employee surveys of banking profesionals in Europe, job listings, expert finance career advice, insider salary information and more.

V/\ULT CAREER LIBRARY 67

analyst finally gets home at 5 a.m., which gives him enough time for a two-hour nap, a shower, and a change of clothes.

Wednesday

Unfortunately, there is a scheduled drafting session out of town on Wednesday relating to another transaction, and the flight is at 8 a.m. Having slept only two hours, the analyst reads his draft of the prospectus on the plane, and arrives with a VP at the law firm's office at 11 a.m., armed with some comments to point out to the group. Many hours and coffees later, the VP and analyst get back on the plane, where the analyst falls dead asleep. After the flight touches down, the analyst returns to the office at 8 p.m. — and continues modeling for a few hours. At midnight, the analyst heads home.

Thursday

The analyst is roped into doing another pitchbook, this one for a merger deal. He frantically works to complete a merger model: gathering information, keying in data, and working with an associate looking over his shoulder. By the time he and the associate have finished the analysis, it is 1 a.m.

Friday

Friday is even worse. The merger model is delivered to the hands of the senior VP overseeing the work, but returned covered in red ink. Changes take the better part of the day, and progress is slow. Projections have to be rejiggered, more research found, and new companies added to the list of comps. At 7 p.m. on Friday, the analyst calls his friends to tell them he won't make it out tonight — again. At 11 p.m., he heads home.

Saturday

Even Saturday requires nearly 10 hours of work, but much of the afternoon the analyst waits by the phone to hear from the VP who is looking at the latest version of the models.

Sunday

No rest on Sunday. This day involves checking some numbers, but the afternoon, thankfully, is completely free for some napping and downtime.

The analyst adds up a total of maybe 90 hours this week. It could have been much worse: at some firms, analysts typically work more than 100 hours per week.

Comps, Illustrated

What exactly are **comps**? You may have heard of comps, or comparable company analysis — and the fact that after two years, analysts never want to do comp analysis ever again.

In short, comps summarize financial market measures of similar companies within an industry group. For example, suppose we wanted to compare a software company (our client, Company C, which is considering a sale of the company to other software companies), Companies A and B. Comps usually are many pages long, but often begin with something like the following.

Last 12 Months Data (£ in millions)

Company	Sales	EBITDA	Net Income	EPS	Stock Price
A	2,800	500	200	£2.00	£75.00
B	900	200	50	£0.65	£18.00
C	3,000	600	195	£1.15	£48.75

Valuation Measures

Company	Shares (millions)	Market Value	Net Debt	Enterprise Value
A	100	7,500	1,450	8,950
B	77	1,385	600	1,985
C	170	8,266	190	8,456

Ratios and Multiples

Company	Ent Value/ Revenue	Ent Value/ EBITDA	Price/ Earning
A	3	18	38
B	2	10	28
C	3	14	42

Here we begin to summarize income statement data, including sales and EPS and build up to market valuation measures and, finally, a few ratios. From this illustration, we could interpret the numbers above as: "Our client (Company C) is the biggest firm in terms of sales, has the most cash flow, and the highest P/E ratio. The high P/E ratio makes Company C the most "expensive" stock, trading at 42 times earnings. Note that EBITDA is often used as a proxy for cash flow. (continued...)

Visit **Vault Europe's Finance Career Channel** at www.Vault.com/Europe for insider firm profiles, employee surveys of banking profesionals in Europe, job listings, expert finance career advice, insider salary information and more.

VAULT CAREER LIBRARY 69

Such analyses help bankers interpret how firms are trading in the market, how they compare to their peers, and what valuations seem typical. Comps are useful for valuing companies going public as well as valuing companies that are acquisition targets. Keep in mind that this is a very simplified version of what true comps look like.

A Day in the Life: Analyst, Investment Banking (UBS)

8:00 a.m.: This is a good time to start for first-year analysts; everyone else comes in a half an hour or an hour later.

8:03 a.m.: Upon entering cube/office, check to see if voice mail light is on. If it's Monday, pray to God it's not on, because that means you didn't check it over the weekend and someone might have had work for you to do and wants it in an hour from now (or worse, wanted it yesterday).

8:05 a.m.: Get hot coffee or tea; you'll need it to wake up. Also, out of camaraderie, get one for other analyst guy who didn't go home in the first place. He'll thank you for it, though he probably won't know your name in his state of stupor.

8:10 a.m.: Check e-mail. Receive a bunch of transaction announcements from all over the world, as well as some newsletter relevant to your industry/group sent out by another analyst to everyone. Unless you're into the latest news on, say, regulatory decisions on telecoms or the roofing equipment industry, it's safe to delete and go on with the remainder of e-mails. E-mail might contain information requests by others in the firm, asking for case studies, connections with certain personnel at client firms, etc. As an analyst, you won't know most of this stuff anyway, so hit delete.

8:30 a.m.: Look nervously around the corner to see if associate or director has arrived, so nobody catches you reading a chapter in that novel you've been trying to finish on the weekends and spare morning hours for the past six months.

9:00 a.m.: Office/floor officially running, phones ringing, workday starts. Greet the assistants. Don't call them secretaries. Make sure they like — so you can avoid a short-lived career.

9:15 a.m.: After waiting for five minutes for slow network to load, find your files and continue on research/model — whatever you didn't finish the night before because you knew you still had this morning.

9:17 a.m.: Phone rings. Director/associate calls you for status on the one thing you haven't finished yet. Hold him off until you can finish it and curse yourself for not finishing up last night.

9:30 a.m.: Phone rings again. You know what director/associate is going to say so right off the bat you say, "I'm almost done." Then in between a lot of "oks" you curse your computer for being so slow.

10:00 a.m.: Conference call with deal team, which may include people from other product and industry groups who work in conjunction on a project with you. Managing director is likely to read over material that you were 90 percent responsible for — but only your associate and director know this. Pray nothing's wrong with numbers and grammar.

11:10 a.m.: Too early for lunch but you're already hungry. What to do before lunch? Put together a few public information books ("PIBs"), work on a pitch book or still try to balance your model, which won't happen because you're too hungry to concentrate.

11:15 a.m.: Call up any other analyst buddy in some other group or office and make small talk. He won't have time to talk to you anyway, but it beats having to look at the model again.

12:30 p.m.: You're really hungry but you must print out some files for your associate/director before you leave, so nobody will come around looking for you when they need the printouts. E-mail only if they ask for it. They'll forget it's there anyway.

12:45 p.m.: Lunch across the street or, if you feel rich, pick up food from some fancy sandwich place a few miles away as a sign of your protest to the cafeteria's overpriced salads. Always take cell phone with you.

1:45 p.m.: Return to work and hope nobody cared that you were gone for an hour.

2:00 p.m.: Try not to fall asleep because of the heavy wrap or potatoes you had for lunch. Drink lots of water. Sit down with associate to talk about some preliminary research he needs you to pull from all kinds of sources. He tells you a few other things and goes off. Take notes so as not to forget a single thing. Best excuse later: "I only did what you told me to." This works only if you really did exactly that. Wait for presentations department to turn around a job you sent with the director's changes. He always has some.

3:00 p.m.: New business coming in through another managing director. Your task, should you accept (and you will), is to fill out the first in a long series of forms that will be submitted to one committee after another for review.

Visit **Vault Europe's Finance Career Channel** at www.Vault.com/Europe for insider firm profiles, employee surveys of banking profesionals in Europe, job listings, expert finance career advice, insider salary information and more.

V/\ULT   CAREER LIBRARY   **71**

Essentially, every form looks the same and involves a "company overview." If this is a form for a credit approval committee for a "risky" company, be prepared to write 75 to 100 pages worth of memo, the contents of which are virtually identical with the company's 10-K. But, it has to be in UBS format ,so you can't just pass along the 10-K. You will agonize over the outline and dig through countless sources to extract information and dump it, re-formatted, into your growing file. This will take the rest of the week if your managing director planned ahead. Otherwise, the loan commitment is due in two days and you will not sleep.

4:30 p.m.: It's fair game that anyone, anywhere, anyplace can walk by or call you up during this time for tasks/chores, like putting together a set of trading/transaction comparables, make more PIBs, do extra research, fetch a few industry reports, download files accessible to everyone on the Internet, make printouts, put together working group lists for deal teams on a transaction, etc. Help out other analysts calling for some files or work you've done on something so they don't have to start from scratch on their related project. Sometimes a managing director calls and asks you something you could not possibly know. Sound as smart as possible and then defer the question to your associate.

6:30 p.m.: Order dinner. At UBS, any dinner ordered before this time is not eligible for refund. Adjust stomach and eating habits accordingly from day one, or suffer irritability and lack of concentration going forward. Everyone asks you to put it on your corporate Amex card. Make sure you have enough on your personal bank balance to pay the full amount when the bill is due later, since your refund through the ubiquitous UBS expense system will take a month to process. Run around with list of who wants what, don't make suggestions, don't write down the wrong thing, and get on with it.

6:35 p.m.: Wait for dinner. (An alternative to waiting might be: A managing director/executive director gives a director a call. The director calls an associate. The associate calls you, and you're evening/week/weekend is ruined because a client wants presentation and model X by the end of next week. The managing director assured the client we'd deliver model X by Monday, "no problem at all." He also said, "While we're at it, we'll also supply Y, Z and A and the reverse of X for two other companies" to further elucidate the issue for the client, who said he really doesn't need all this. But after gentle insistence by the managing director, the client consents, and is glad he went with an ambitious firm such as UBS. After the director gives last instructions to associate or you, then wait for dinner.)

7:45 p.m.: Eat dinner, chat with other analysts about what's up. Take great interest in rumors, gossip and all kinds of BS that would get you fired if you spoke about it outside the conference room you're all huddled in.

8:35 p.m.: Return to work. Call up internal library for some research you don't have access to and hope someone's still there, or it will be a tight morning tomorrow.

10:00 p.m.: Associate leaves, giving you a couple more things to do on way out. "Take your time, no rush," he assures and thanks you for the good job you've been doing in advance. You appreciate his gratitude but would also like to go home at some point.

11:00 p.m.: Discounted cash flow model inputs take very long and the model still doesn't balance. It will be a long night.

2:00 a.m.: You check your e-mail one more time (in fact, you never close it in the first place, as this is the first rule of survival for anyone in investment banking), then you make sure everything is saved, and log out the computer. Call a car and get some sleep.

Associates

With a role similar to analysts, associates are primarily responsible for financial models and pitchbooks. A week for an associate (especially a first-year associate) might resemble closely the scenario painted above, with oversight duties over analysts working on models for the associate. In addition, the associate may be more involved in dealing with the MDs and in checking pitchbooks before they are sent out.

A more experienced associate will sit down more frequently with a VP or MD, going over details of potential deals or discussing numbers. In contrast to analysts, who work as generalists, associates typically focus on one specific industry. One week for an analyst might include deals for a steel company, a high-tech company, and a restaurant company; an associate will typically focus on an industry like high tech or health care. However, like analysts, associates must work carefully and thoughtfully and put in long hours to gain the respect of their supervisors.

Visit **Vault Europe's Finance Career Channel** at **www.Vault.com/Europe** for insider firm profiles, employee surveys of banking profesionals in Europe, job listings, expert finance career advice, insider salary information and more.

V/\ULT CAREER LIBRARY 73

A Day in the Life: Associate, Investment Banking (Goldman Sachs)

8:30 a.m.: Get in. Check e-mail and voice mail.

9:00 a.m.: Breakfast with summer associates "to see how they're doing."

10:00 a.m.: A couple of conference calls with clients that are usually "30-minute phone meetings talking about what I'm planning on presenting to clients next week, and to find out what other topics I should discuss. We basically share ideas."

11:00 a.m.: E-mailing results of conference call meeting to MDs.

11:30 a.m.: Meet with analysts to assign them work. ("I usually give work to full-time analysts and let them run with it. For summer analysts, I'll make sure they're getting a good perspective and are learning. I'll also make sure I'm giving them enough to test them to see if they get it, and have what it takes to be a full-time analyst.)

12:30 p.m.: Lunch. ("About four days a week I grab a sandwich at a deli and eat it at my desk. Sometimes, with a group of people, I eat at the cafeteria, which is pretty good. They recently redid the cafeteria. It used to be a dump.")**1:30 p.m.:** Conference call with a Goldman MD and a client's CEO about meeting next week.

3:00 p.m.: Prepare reports based on call for meetings next week.

6:30 p.m.: Meet with analysts to dole out work such as research and financial modeling.

7:00 p.m.: Order dinner and eat with a few other people in the office.

8:00 p.m.: Continue on reports for tomorrow's and next week's meetings.

12:00 a.m.: Call car and head home. ("When you leave all depends. On average I leave around midnight, but it's not uncommon to leave after 1 a.m. And sometimes, not often but during slow times, I'll leave as early as 7:30 p.m. or 8:00 p.m.. Third-year associates work between 10 and 20 hours collectively on the weekends. For first and second-year associates, it's pretty much a full-time job.")

> *Overall, what Goldman does exceptionally well is create a team culture. And what that really means is people respect young bankers' opinions and look out for the development of junior bankers. Juniors' opinions count and everyone's included on calls. Analysts and associates are encouraged to contribute. They're not locked in a room running numbers. People expect you to have an opinion. It's a place where people have a very low tolerance for egos and obnoxious behavior. There's no yelling and screaming."*
>
> *— Goldman Sachs insider*

Vice Presidents and MDs (a.k.a. "Bankers")

As you become a banker, you begin to shift from modeling and number crunching to relationship building. This gradual transition happens during the senior associate phase as the associate begins interfacing with existing clients. Ultimately, VPs and MDs spend most of their time and energy finding new clients and servicing existing clients. VPs spend more time managing associates and analysts and the pitchbook creation process than MDs, but their responsibilities begin to resemble those of MDs at the senior VP level. The typical week for a VP or MD, then, looks quite different from that of an analyst or associate.

Monday

The banker gets a courier package delivered at 6 a.m. at her house, and carries this with her to the airport. The package contains several copies of an M&A pitch that she intends to make that day. Her team put the finishing touches on the analysis just a few hours before, while she slept at home. Her schedule that day includes three meetings in Houston and one important pitch in the afternoon. As an oil and gas banker, the banker finds she spend two-thirds of her time flying to Texas and Louisiana, where her clients are clustered. In her morning sales calls, the banker visits with a couple CEOs of different companies, gives them an updated general pitchbook and discusses their businesses and whether they have upcoming financing needs. The third meeting of the day is a lunch meeting with a CFO from a company she led a deal for last year.

The banker's cell phone seems glued to her head as she drives from meeting to meeting, but she turns it off for her final meeting — an M&A pitch to a CEO of an oilfield service company. Afterward, the banker grabs dinner with the company's CFO, and finds her way to her hotel around 9 p.m.

Visit **Vault Europe's Finance Career Channel** at www.Vault.com/Europe for insider firm profiles, employee surveys of banking profesionals in Europe, job listings, expert finance career advice, insider salary information and more.

V∧ULT CAREER LIBRARY

75

Tuesday

The next day the banker heads to a drafting session at the offices of a law firm downtown. She had gotten up early to read through and review the draft of the prospectus, and made comments in the margins. As her firm is only the co-manager on the deal, she merely brings up issues for the group to consider, and does not lead the discussion, leaving that to the lead manager. After the drafting session, the banker catches an early afternoon flight home, leaving an associate at the drafting session to cover for her.

Wednesday

Back in the office, the banker spends all day on the phone. Flooded with calls, the banker has no time to look at any of the models dropped off in her in-box. Finally, around 6 p.m., she calls the associate and analyst team building an IPO model into her office. For an hour, they go through the numbers, with the banker pointing out problems and missing data items. The associate and analyst leave with a full plate of work ahead. The banker heads home at 8 p.m.

Thursday

The banker is back in the office in the morning to review more models and take some phone calls, but she leaves around noon to catch a flight to make it to a "closing dinner" in Texas. It is time to celebrate one of her successfully managed transactions (it was a follow-on) with the working group. As the lead manager, the banker makes sure that she has plenty of gag gifts for the management team and war stories from the offering to share with the group.

Friday

The banker plans on staying in town to make a few sales visits in the morning. Armed again with pitchbooks, the banker spends a few hours wooing potential clients by discussing merger ideas, financing alternatives and any other relevant transaction that could lead to a fee. Heading home, the banker touches base with her favorite associate to discuss a few models that need work, and what she needs for Monday.

Weekend

Over the weekend, the banker has models couriered to her home, where she goes over the numbers and calls in or messengers her comments and changes to the associate back at the office.

Formulas For Success

The formula for succeeding in banking depends on your role, but some generalizations can be made. The expected qualities of hard work, confidence and dedication ring true in every job, but corporate finance takes these expectations to the nth degree.

Analysts

For the analyst, it is all about keeping your head in the computer, working long hours, and double-checking your work before showing it to bankers. Nothing angers a time-constrained VP more than a young naive analyst who puts together subpar work. Quality of work is key to establishing respect early on, and bankers respect number crunchers who make few mistakes and are not afraid to ask smart, to-the-point questions pertaining to a particular assignment. And, while face time is officially rejected at every bank, bankers tend to frown upon analysts gone before dinner time. A new analyst's best move is to ease into a stressful environment by working hard and learning the ropes as quickly as possible.

Generally, analyst programs last two years although some analysts are invited to stay a third year. Then, graduating analysts often leave to attend graduate school or to find another job. In rare cases, an analyst may be promoted directly to associate, bypassing grad school entirely. The experience is not all gloom and doom, as analysts receive a fast-track learning experience in the City and on Wall Street, top bonuses, and admission to some of the best business schools in the country. Depending on the firm, City analysts either join a specific industry or product group, or fall into a category called generalists, which means that they work on deals and pitchbooks for a variety of industry groups and hence learn about a variety of companies in a range of industries.

Associates

New MBA, law, or other grad-school graduates begin as associates. The associate excels by demonstrating an aptitude to learn quickly, work hard, and establish himself or herself early on as a dedicated group member. At the associate level, placement into an industry group typically occurs soon after the training program ends, although some firms such as Salomon Smith Barney offer generalist programs for an extended period. Impressions can form quickly, and a new group member who shows willingness to work hard and late for a group will create a positive impression. Associates are more involved than analysts in client meetings, due diligence meetings, drafting sessions and roadshows. So, associates must be able to socialize with clients well.

Visit **Vault Europe's Finance Career Channel** at **www.Vault.com/Europe** for insider firm profiles, employee surveys of banking profesionals in Europe, job listings, expert finance career advice, insider salary information and more.

VAULT CAREER LIBRARY   **77**

Over time, associates spend more time on the road, and supervisors keep an eye on their manner and carriage in front of clients. Sharp comments, confidence and poise in front of clients will at this point do more for an associate than all-nighters and face time. Like analysts, associates have also benefited from the recent dearth of talented candidates at investment banks. The promotion time from associate to vice president has recently been shorted at many firms. Several I-banks have also started to offer private equity investment opportunities to associates — opportunities which were previously available only to officers of the firm (vice presidents or higher). Typically, associates move up to vice president level within three to five years.

Vice Presidents

Depending on the firm, VPs often succeed by showing good managerial skills over deals and transactions, as well as over analysts and associates. VPs ultimately are responsible for pitchbooks, transaction details and therefore become managers both in and out of the office. Organization, attention to detail, and strong motivational skills lead to big-sized bonuses. Most important however, is a demonstration of leadership. VPs must win business, convince clients to go ahead with certain deals, handle meetings effectively, and cover for MDs at all times. At regional I-banks, the ability to generate business reigns supreme over other characteristics, whereas Wall Street VPs tend to be transaction processors, who complete deals handed to them.

Managing Directors

Success for an MD comes with industry knowledge, an ability to handle clients, and an ability to find new ones. The MD's most important task includes schmoozing in the industry, finding potential deals, and pitching them with confidence and poise. Public speaking skills, industry awareness, demonstrated experience and an ability to sell combine to create the best bankers. Importantly, however, MDs must still be able to grasp the numbers side of the business and be able to explain them to clients. The progression from associate to MD is typically an eight- to 10-year track.

Institutional Sales and Trading (S&T)

CHAPTER 9

The war zone

If you've ever been to an investment banking trading floor, you've witnessed the chaos. It's usually a lot of swearing, yelling and flashing computer screens: a pressure cooker of stress. Sometimes the floor is a quiet rumble of activity, but when the market takes a nosedive, panic ensues and the volume kicks up a notch. Traders must rely on their market instincts, and salespeople yell for bids when the market tumbles. Deciding what to buy or sell, and at what price to buy and sell, is difficult when millions of dollars at stake.

However, salespeople and traders work much more reasonable hours than research analysts or corporate finance bankers. Rarely does a salesperson or trader venture into the office on a Saturday or Sunday; the trading floor is completely devoid of life on weekends. Any corporate finance analyst who has crossed a trading floor on a Saturday will tell you that the only noise to be heard on the floor is the clocks ticking every minute and the whir of the air conditioner.

Shop Talk

Here's a quick example of how a salesperson and a trader interact on an emerging market bond trade.

SALESPERSON: Receives a call from a buy-side firm (say, a large mutual fund). The buy-side firm wishes to sell $10 million of a particular Mexican Par government-issued bond (denominated in U.S. dollars). The emerging markets bond salesperson, seated next to the emerging markets traders, stands up in his chair and yells to the relevant trader, "Give me a bid on $10 million Mex Par, six and a quarter, nineteens."

TRADER: "I got 'em at 73 and an eighth."

Translation: I am willing to buy them at a price of $73.125 per $100 of face value. As mentioned, the $10 million represents amount of par value the client wanted to sell, meaning the trader will buy the bonds, paying 73.125 percent of $10 million *plus accrued interest (to factor in interest earned between interest payments).*

SALESPERSON: "Can't you do any better than that?"

Translation: Please buy at a higher price, as I will get a higher commission.

Visit **Vault Europe's Finance Career Channel** at www.Vault.com/Europe for insider firm profiles, employee surveys of banking profesionals in Europe, job listings, expert finance career advice, insider salary information and more.

VAULT CAREER LIBRARY 79

> **TRADER:** "That's the best I can do. The market is falling right now. You want to sell?"
>
> **SALESPERSON:** "Done. $10 million."

S&T: A symbiotic relationship?

Institutional sales and trading are highly dependent on one another. The propaganda that you read in glossy firm brochures portrays those in sales and trading as a shiny, happy integrated team environment of professionals working for the client's interests. While often that is true, salespeople and traders frequently clash, disagree, and bicker.

Simply put, salespeople provide the clients for traders, and traders provide the products for sales. Traders would have nobody to trade for without sales, but sales would have nothing to sell without traders. Understanding how a trader makes money and how a salesperson makes money should explain how conflicts can arise.

Traders make money by selling high and buying low (this difference is called the spread). They are buying stocks or bonds for clients, and these clients filter in through sales. A trader faced with a buy order for a buy-side firm could care less about the performance of the securities once they are sold. He or she just cares about making the spread. In a sell trade, this means selling at the highest price possible. In a buy trade, this means buying at the lowest price possible.

The salesperson, however, has a different incentive. The total return on the trade often determines the money a salesperson makes, so he wants the trader to sell at a low price. The salesperson also wants to be able to offer the client a better price than competing firms in order to get the trade and earn a commission. This of course leads to many interesting situations, and at the extreme, salespeople and traders who eye one another suspiciously.

The personalities

Salespeople possess remarkable communication skills, including outgoing personalities and a smoothness not often seen in traders. Traders sometimes call them bullshit artists while salespeople counter by calling traders quant guys with no personality. Traders are tough, quick, and often consider themselves smarter than salespeople. The salespeople probably know better how to have fun, but the traders win the prize for mental sharpness and the ability to handle stress.

Trading — The Basics

Trading can make or break an investment bank. Without traders to execute buy and sell transactions, no public deal would get done, no liquidity would exist for securities, and no commissions or spreads would accrue to the bank. Traders carry a "book" accounting for the daily revenue that they generate for the firm — down to the dollar.

Liquidity

As discussed earlier, liquidity is the ability to find tradeable securities in the market. When a large number of buyers and sellers co-exist in the market, a stock or bond is said to be highly liquid. Let's take a look at the liquidity of various types of securities.

- **Common stock**. For stock, liquidity depends on the stock's float in the market. Float is the number of shares available for trade in the market (not the total number of shares, which may include unregistered stock) times the stock price. Usually over time, as a company grows and issues more stock, its float and liquidity increase.

- **Debt**. Debt, or bonds, is another story, however. For debt issues, corporate bonds typically have the most liquidity immediately following the placement of the bonds. After a few months, most bonds trade infrequently, ending up in a few big money managers' portfolios for good. If buyers and sellers want to trade corporate debt, the lack of liquidity will mean that buyers will be forced to pay a liquidity premium, or sellers will be forced to accept a liquidity discount.

- **Government issues**. Government bonds are yet another story. Munis, treasuries, agencies, and other government bonds form an active market with better liquidity than that of corporate bonds. In fact, the largest single traded security in the world is the 30-year U.S. Government bond (known as the Long Bond), although the 10-year note is closing in fast.

Trading and traders

Trading of financial securities and derivatives is conducted either over-the-counter (OTC) or through exchanges. In the OTC markets trading is conducted by screen or telephone on the basis of bank-to-bank dealing. The main OTC markets are the massive foreign exchange market, the interbank market for short-term deposits, the bullion market, Nasdaq and the international bond market.

Visit **Vault Europe's Finance Career Channel** at **www.Vault.com/Europe** for insider firm profiles, employee surveys of banking profesionals in Europe, job listings, expert finance career advice, insider salary information and more.

VAULT CAREER LIBRARY 81

Stock exchanges are member organisations with buildings, rule books, standard contract units, settlement dates and delivery specifications. All the European stock exchanges are now electronic markets. Traders operate through computerised dealing systems from dealing rooms at the banks for which they work.

In the U.S., the NYSE and the Chicago commodities and derivatives exchanges continue to use floor trading as well as electronic dealing. At the NYSE, the trading floor bustles with activity as stocks and bonds are traded and auctioned back and forth by floor traders. In fact, these traders are really floor brokers, who follow through with the execution of a stock or bond transaction. Floor brokers receive their orders from traders working at the offices of investment banks or brokerage firms, handling orders from salespeople and investors. We will cover the mechanics of a trade later. First, let's discuss the basics of how a trader makes money and carries inventory.

How the trader makes money

Understanding how traders make money is simple. As discussed earlier, traders buy stocks and bonds at a low price, then sell them for a slightly higher price. This difference is called the **bid-ask spread**, or, simply, the spread. For example, a bond may be quoted at 99 1/2 bid, 99 5/8 ask. Money managers who wish to buy this bond would have to pay the ask price to the trader, or 99 5/8. It is likely that the trader purchased the bond earlier at 99 1/2, from an investor looking to sell his securities. Therefore, the trader earns the bid-ask spread on a buy/sell transaction. The bid-ask spread here is 1/8 of a dollar, or $0.125, per $100 of bonds. If the trader bought and sold 10,000 bonds (which each have $1,000 face value for a total value of $100 million), the spread earned would amount to $125,000 for the trader. Not bad for a couple of trades.

Spreads vary depending on the security sold. Generally speaking, the more liquidity a stock or bond has, the narrower the spread. Government bonds (also referred to as sovereign bonds), the most liquid of all securities, typically trade at spreads of a mere 1/128th of a dollar. That is, a $1,000 trade nets only 78 cents for the trader. However, government bonds (sometimes called govies for short) trade in huge volumes. So, a $100 million govie trade nets $78,125 to the investment bank — not a bad trade.

Inventory

While the concept of how a trader makes money (the bid-ask spread) is eminently simple, actually executing this strategy is a different story. Traders are subject to market movements — bond and stock prices fluctuate constantly. Because the trader's ultimate responsibility is simply to buy low and sell high, this means anticipating and reacting appropriately to dynamic market conditions that often catch even the most experienced people off guard. A trader who has bought securities but has not sold them is said to be carrying **inventory**.

Suppose, for instance, that a trader purchased stock at €52 7/8, the market bid price, from a money manager selling his stock. The ask was €53 when the trade was executed. Now the trader looks to unload the stock. The trader has committed the firm's money to purchase stock, and therefore has what is called price movement risk. What happens if the stock price falls before she can unload at the current ask price of €53? Obviously, the trader and the firm lose money. Because of this risk, traders attempt to ensure that the bid-ask spread has enough cushion so that when a stock falls, they do not lose money.

The problem with carrying inventory is that security prices can move dramatically. A company announcing bad news may cause such a rush of sell orders that the price may drop significantly. Remember, every trade has two sides, a buyer and a seller. If the price of a stock or bond is falling, the only buyers in the market may be the traders making a market in that security (as opposed to individual investors). These market makers have to judge by instinct and market savvy where to offer to buy the stock back from investors. If they buy at too high a price (a price higher than the trader can sell the stock back for), they can lose big. Banks will lose even more if a stock falls while a trader holds that stock in inventory.

So what happens in a widespread free-falling market? Well, you can just imagine the pandemonium on the trading floor as investors rush to sell their securities however possible. Traders and investors carrying inventory all lose money. At that point, no one knows where the market will bottom out.

On the flip side, in a booming market, carrying inventory consistently leads to making money. In fact, it is almost impossible not to. Any stock or bond held on the books overnight appreciates in value the next day in a strong bull market. This can foster an environment in which poor decisions become overlooked because of the steady upward climb of the markets. Traders buy and sell securities as investors demand. Usually, a trader owns a stock or bond, ready to sell when asked. When a trader owns the security, he is said to be **long** the security (what we previously called carrying inventory). This is easy enough to understand.

Being long or short

Consider the following, though. Suppose an investor wished to buy a security and called a trader who at the time did not have the security in inventory. In this case, the trader can

Visit **Vault Europe's Finance Career Channel** at www.Vault.com/Europe for insider firm profiles, employee surveys of banking profesionals in Europe, job listings, expert finance career advice, insider salary information and more.

V/\ULT CAREER LIBRARY **83**

do one of two things — 1) not execute the trade or 2) sell the security, despite the fact that he or she does not own it.

How does the second scenario work? The trader goes short the security by selling it to the investor without owning it. Where does he get the security? By borrowing the security from someone else.

Let's look at an example. Suppose a client wished to buy 10,000 shares of Microsoft (MSFT) stock, but the trader did not have any MSFT stock to sell. The trader likely would sell shares to the client by borrowing them from elsewhere and doing what is called **short-selling**, or shorting. In such a short transaction, the trader must eventually buy 10,000 shares back of MSFT to replace the shares he borrowed. The trader will then look for sellers of MSFT in the broker-dealer market, and will often indicate to salespeople of his need to buy MSFT shares. (Salespeople may even seek out their clients who own MSFT, checking to see if they would be willing to sell the stock.)

The problems with shorting or short-selling stock are the opposite of those that one faces by owning the stock. In a long position, traders worry about big price drops — as the value of your inventory declines, you lose money. In a short position, a trader worries that the stock increases in price. He has locked in his selling price upfront, but has not locked in his purchase price. If the price of the stock moves up, then the purchase price moves up as well.

Tracking the trades

Traders keep track of the exact details of every trade they make. Trading assistants often perform this function, detailing the transaction (buy or sell), the amount (number of shares or bonds), the price, the buyer/seller, and the time of the trade. At the end of the day, the compilation of the dollars made/lost for that day is called a profit and loss statement, or **P&L**. The P&L statement is all-important to a trader: daily, weekly, monthly, quarterly — traders know the status of their P&L's for these periods at any given time.

Types of trades

Unbeknownst to most people, traders actually work in two different markets, that is, they buy and sell securities for two different types of customers.

• One is the **inside market**, which is a monopoly market made up only of broker-dealers. Traders actually utilize a special broker screen that posts the prices broker-dealers are willing to buy and sell to each other. This works as an important source of liquidity when a trader needs to buy or sell securities.

- The other is **outside market**, composed of outside customers an investment bank transacts with. These include a diverse range of money managers and investors, or the firm's outside clients. Traders earn the bulk of their profits in the outside market.

Not only do traders at investment banks work in two different markets, but they can make two different types of trades. As mentioned earlier, these include:

- **Client trades.** These are simply trades done on the behest of outside customers. Most traders' jobs are to make a market in a security for the firm's clients. They buy and sell as market forces dictate and pocket the bid-ask spread along the way. The vast majority of traders trade for clients.

- **Proprietary trades.** Sometimes traders are given leeway in terms of what securities they may buy and sell for the firm. Using firm capital, proprietary traders, or prop traders as they are often called, actually trade not to fulfill client demand for stocks and bonds, but to make bets on the market. Some prop traders trade such obscure things as the yield curve, making bets as the direction that the yield curve will move. Other are arbitragers, who follow the markets and lock in arbitrage profit when market inefficiencies develop. (In a simple example, a market inefficiency would occur if a security, say U.S. government bonds, is trading for different prices in different locales, say in the U.S. vs. the UK. Actual market inefficiencies these days often involve derivatives and currency exchange rates.)

A Trader's Cockpit

You may have wondered about the pile of computer gear a trader uses. This impressive mess of technology, which includes half a dozen blinking monitors, represents more technology per square inch than that used by any other professional in the City or on Wall Street. Each trader utilizes different information sources, and so has different computer screens sprouting out data and news. Typically, though, a Wall Street trader has the following:

- **Bloomberg machine:** Bloombergs were invented originally only as bond calculators. (The company that makes them was founded by a former Salomon Brothers trader, Mike Bloomberg, now a billionaire who owns a media empire.) Today, however, they perform so many intricate and complex functions that they've become ubiquitous on any equity or debt

Visit **Vault Europe's Finance Career Channel** at www.Vault.com/Europe for insider firm profiles, employee surveys of banking profesionals in Europe, job listings, expert finance career advice, insider salary information and more.

VAULT CAREER LIBRARY

85

trading floor. In a few quick keystrokes, a trader can access a bond's price, yield, rating, duration, convexity, and literally thousands of other tidbits. Market news, stock information and even e-mail reside real-time on the Bloomberg.

- **Phone monitor:** Traders' phone systems are almost as complex as the Bloombergs. The phones consist of a touch-screen monitor with a cluster of phone lines. There are multiple screens that a trader can flip to, with direct dialing and secured lines designed to ensure a foolproof means of communicating with investors, floor brokers, salespeople and the like. For example, one Morgan Stanley associate tells of a direct phone line to billionaire George Soros.

- **Small broker screens:** These include monitors posting market prices from other broker-dealers, or investment banks. Traders deal with each other to facilitate client needs and provide a forum for the flow of securities.

- **Large Sun monitor:** Typically divided into numerous sections, the Sun monitor can be tailored to the trader's needs. Popular pages include U.S. Treasury markets, bond market data, news pages and equity prices.

Executing a Trade

If you are a retail investor, and call your broker to place an order, how is the trade actually executed? Now that we know the basics of the trading business, we will cover the mechanics of how stocks or bonds are actually traded. We will begin with what is called **small lots trading**, or the trading of relatively small amounts of a security.

Small lots trading

Surprising to many people, the process of completing a small lot transaction differs depending on where the security is traded and what type of security it is. In the U.S. the pattern is as follows:

• For an NYSE-traded stock, the transaction begins with an investor placing the order and ends with the actual transaction being executed on the floor of the New York Stock Exchange. Here, the trade is a physical, as opposed to an electronic one.

• For Nasdaq-traded stocks, the transaction typically originates with an investor placing an order with a broker and ends with that broker selling stock from his current inventory of securities (stocks the broker actually owns). An excellent analogy of this type of market, called an Over-the-Counter (OTC) Market, is that a trader acts like a pawn shop, selling an inventory of securities when a buyer desires, just like the pawn shop owner sells a watch to a store visitor. And, when an investor wishes to sell securities, he or she contacts a trader who willingly purchases them at a price dictated by the trader, just like the pawn shop owner gives prices at which he will buy watches. (As in a pawn shop, the trader makes money through the difference between the buying and selling price, the bid-ask spread.) In the OTC scenario, the actual storage of the securities is electronic, residing inside the trader's computer.

• For bonds, transactions rarely occur in small lots. By convention, most bonds have a face value of $1,000, and orders for one or even 10 bonds are not common. However, the execution of the trade is similar to Nasdaq stocks. Traders carry inventory on their computer and buy and sell on the spot without the need for an NYSE-style trading pit.

The following pages illustrate the execution of a trade on both the Nasdaq and the NYSE stock exchanges. A bond transaction works similarly to a Nasdaq trade.

Here's a look at the actions that take place during a trade of a Nasdaq-listed stock.

Nasdaq

ORDER: You call in an order of 1,000 shares of Microsoft stock to your retail broker. For small orders, you agree on a trade placed at the market. That is, you say you are willing to pay the ask price as it is currently trading in the market.

EXECUTION: First, the retail broker calls the appropriate trader to handle the transaction. The Nasdaq trader, called a market maker, carries an inventory of certain stocks available for purchase.

TRANSACTION: The market maker checks his inventory of stock. If he carries the security, he simply makes the trade, selling the 1,000 shares of Microsoft from his account (the market maker's account) to you. If he does not already own the stock, then he will buy 1,000 shares directly from another market maker and then sell them immediately to you at a slightly higher price than he paid for them.

Visit **Vault Europe's Finance Career Channel** at **www.Vault.com/Europe** for insider firm profiles, employee surveys of banking profesionals in Europe, job listings, expert finance career advice, insider salary information and more.

VAULT CAREER LIBRARY

87

Here's a look at a trade of a stock listed on the New York Stock Exchange.

NYSE

ORDER: You decide to buy 1,000 shares of GE. You contact your broker and give an order to buy 1,000 shares. The broker tells you the last trade price (65 1/2) and the current quote (65 3/8 bid, 65 5/8 ask) and takes your order to buy 1,000 shares at the market. The broker also notes the volume of stock available for buy and sell, currently 500 X 500 (i.e., 500 shares of GE in demand at the bid and 500 shares of GE available for sale at the ask).

TRANSMITTAL TO THE FLOOR: The order is transmitted from the broker at the I-bank through the NYSE's computer network directly to what are called NYSE specialists (see sidebar) handling the stock.

THE TRADE: The specialist's book displays a new order to buy 1,000 shares of XYZ at the market. At this point, the specialist can fill the order himself from his own account at the last trade price of 65 1/2, or alternatively, he can transact the 1,000 shares trade at 65 5/8. In the latter case, 500 shares would come from the public customer (who had 500 shares of stock available at the bid price) and 500 shares would come from the specialist selling from his own account.

THE TRADE FINALIZED: If the floor specialist elects to trade at 65 5/8, he sends the details of the trade to his back office via the Exchange's computer network and also electronically to the brokerage firm. This officially records the transaction.

U.S. and European Stock Exchanges

The New York Stock Exchange (NYSE) is the world's biggest securities exchange, with around 2,800 listed stocks and a market capitalisation ot $13 trillion. Its physical and often flamboyant trading floor is located at the corner of Wall Street and Broad Street in lower Manhattan. By contrast, Nasdaq, the second U.S. stock market, has no physical location being a virtual trading arena. Approved Nasdaq dealers make a market in particular stocks by buying and selling shares through a computerized trading system. This is called an over-the-counter system or OTC system, with a network of linked computers acting as the auctioneer.

The London Stock Exchange (LSE) is Europe's premier stock exchange and the fourth largest in the world after New York, Nasdaq and Tokyo. The shares of around 2,500 British companies are quoted on the LSE with a combined market capitalisation of $2.8 trillion plus around 350 overseas companies with primary or secondary listings. Dealing on the LSE is conducted through two alternative types of trading system. SEAQ (Stock Exchange Automated Quotations) is a *quote-driven* trading system, being a continuously updated electronic board of buy and sell prices for UK and overseas shares. SETS (Stock Exchange Electronic Trading Service) is an *order-driven* trading system, based on an electronic order book that matches buy and sell orders and executes them automatically.

Europe's second most important stock exchange is Paris-based Euronext, a merger of the Amsterdam, Brussels, Paris, Lisbon and Milan stock exchanges formed in 2000. The market capitalisation of shares quoted on Euronext is $2.3 trillion. Euronext also owns LIFFE (London International Financial Futures and Options Exchange) Europe's premier financial derivatives exchange.

Germany was slow to develop an equities culture because of the traditional role of the major domestic banks in the provision of corporate funding and their substantial shareholdings. The market capitalisation of companies quoted on the Deutsche Borse is $1.1 trillion, less than half the London or Paris-based exchanges. In recent years the Deutsche Borse has argued that an amalgamation with the LSE would provide economies of scale and a counterbalance to Euronext, but the LSE rejected its advances.

Visit **Vault Europe's Finance Career Channel** at www.Vault.com/Europe for insider firm profiles, employee surveys of banking profesionals in Europe, job listings, expert finance career advice, insider salary information and more.

VAULT CAREER LIBRARY　89

Block trades

Small trades placed through brokers (often called **retail trades**) require a few simple entries into a computer. In these cases, traders record the exchange of a few hundred shares or a few thousand shares, and the trade happens with a few swift keystrokes.

However, when a large institutional investor seeks to buy or sell a large chunk of stock, or a block of stock, the sheer size of the order involves additional facilitation. A buy order for 200,000 shares of IBM stock, for instance, would not easily be accomplished without a block trader. At any given moment, only so much stock is available for sale, and to buy a large quantity would drive the price up in the market (to entice more sellers into the market to sell).

For a NYSE stock, the process of **block trading** is similar to that of any small buy or sell order. The difference is that a small trade arrives electronically to the specialist on the floor of the exchange, while a block trade runs through a floor broker, who then hand-delivers the order to the specialist. The style of a block trade also differs, depending on the client's wishes. Some block trades are done at the market and some block trades involve working the order.

- **At the market.** Say Fidelity wishes to buy 200,000 shares of IBM, and they first contact the block trader at an investment bank. If Fidelity believed that IBM stock was moving up, they would indicate that the purchase of the shares should occur at the market. In this case, the trader would call the floor broker (in reality, he contacts the floor broker's clerk), to tell him or her to buy the next available 200,000 shares of IBM. The clerk delivers the ticket to the floor broker, who then takes it to the specialist dealing in IBM stock. Again, the specialist acts as an auctioneer, matching sellers to the IBM buyer. Once the floor broker accumulates the entire amount of stock, likely from many sellers, his or her clerk is sent back to the phones to call back the trader. The final trading price is a weighted average of all of the purchase prices from the individual sellers.

- **Working the order.** Alternately, if Fidelity believes that IBM was going to bounce around in price, they might ask the trader to work the order in order to hopefully get a better price than what is currently in the market. The trader then would call the floor broker and indicate that he or she should work at finding as low a price as possible. In this case, the floor broker might linger at the IBM trading post, watching for sell orders to come in, hoping to accumulate the shares at as low a price as possible.

Trading bonds

Bond trading takes place in OTC fashion, just as stocks do on the Nasdaq. That is, there is no physical trading floor for bonds, merely a collection of linked computers and market makers around the world (literally). As such, there is no central open outcry market floor for bonds, as there is for NYSE stocks. Therefore, for bond orders, the transaction flow is similar to that of an OTC stock. A buyer calls a broker-dealer, indicates the bonds he wishes to buy, and the trader sells the securities with a phone call and a few keystrokes on his computer.

Visit **Vault Europe's Finance Career Channel** at www.Vault.com/Europe for insider firm profiles, employee surveys of banking profesionals in Europe, job listings, expert finance career advice, insider salary information and more.

VAULT CAREER LIBRARY 91

Trading - The Players

Each desk on a trading floor carries its own sub-culture. Some are tougher than others, some work late, and some socialize outside of work on a regular basis. While some new associates in trading maintain ambitions of working on a particular desk because of the product (say, equities or high yield debt), most find themselves in an environment where they most enjoy the people. After all, salespeople and traders sit side-by-side for 10 hours a day. Liking the guy in the next chair takes precedence when placing an associate full-time on a desk, especially considering the levels of stress, noise and pressure on a trading floor.

The desk

Different areas on the trading floor at an I-bank typically are divided into groups called "**desks**." Common desks include OTC equity trading, Big Board (NYSE) equity trading, convertibles (or "converts"), municipal bonds ("munis"), high yield, and Treasuries. This list is far from complete — some of the bigger firms have 50 or more distinct trading desks on the floor (depending how they are defined). Investment banks usually separate the equity trading floor from the fixed income trading floor. In fact, equity traders and debt traders rarely interact. Conversely, sales and trading within one of these departments are combined and integrated as much as possible. For example, treasury salespeople and treasury traders work next to one another on the same desk. Sales will be covered in following sections.

The players

The players in the trading game depend on the firm. There are no hard and fast rules regarding whether or not one needs an MBA in trading. The degree itself, though less applicable directly to the trading position, tends to matter beyond the trader level. Managers (heads of desks) and higher-ups are often selected from the MBA ranks.

Generally, regional I-banks hire clerks and/or trading assistants (non-MBAs) who are sometimes able to advance to a full-fledged trading job within a few years. Other banks, like Merrill Lynch and others on Wall Street, hire analysts and associates just as they do in investment banking. Thus an analyst job on Wall Street in trading includes a two- to three-year stint before the expectation of going back to business school, and the associate position begins after one earns his or her MBA. The ultimate job in trading is to become a full-fledged trader or a manager over a trading desk. Here we break out the early positions into those more common at regional I-banks and those more common on Wall Street.

Entry-level positions

Regional Frameworks — Traditional Programs

Clerks. The bottom rung of the ladder in trading in regional firms, clerks generally balance the books, tracking a desk or a particular trader's buy and sell transactions throughout the day. A starting point for an undergrad aiming to move up to an assistant trader role, clerks gain exposure to the trading floor environment, the traders themselves and the markets. However, clerks take messages, make copies, go get coffee, and are hardly respected by traders. And at bigger firms, this position can be a dead-end job: clerks may remain in these roles indefinitely, while new MBAs move into full-time trading positions or graduates of top colleges move into real analyst jobs.

Trading assistants. Typically filled by recent graduates of undergraduate universities, the trading assistant position is more involved in trades than the clerk position. Trading assistants move beyond staring at the computer and balancing the books to become more involved with the actual traders. Backing up accounts, relaying messages and reports to and from the floor of the NYSE, and actually speaking with some accounts occasionally — these responsibilities bring trading assistants much closer to understanding how the whole biz works. Depending on the firm, some undergrads immediately move into a trading assistant position with the hope of moving into a full-time trading job.

Note: Clerks and trading assistants at some firms are hired with the possibility of upward advancement, although promoting non-MBAs to full-time trading jobs is becoming more and more uncommon, even at regional firms.

Wall Street Analyst and Associate Programs

Analysts. Similar to corporate finance analysts, trading analysts at Wall Street firms typically are smart undergraduates with the desire to either become a trader or learn about the trading environment. Quantitative skills are a must for analysts, as much of their time is spent dealing with books of trades and numbers. The ability to crunch numbers in a short time is especially important on the fixed income side. Traders often demand bond price or yield calculations with only a moment's notice, and analysts must be able to produce. After a two- to three-year stint, analysts move on to business school or go to another firm, although promotion to the associate level is much more common in trading than it is in corporate finance. (Salaries mirror those paid to corporate finance analysts.)

Visit **Vault Europe's Finance Career Channel** at www.Vault.com/Europe for insider firm profiles, employee surveys of banking profesionals in Europe, job listings, expert finance career advice, insider salary information and more.

VAULT   CAREER LIBRARY   93

Associates. Trading associates, typically recent business school graduates, begin in either rotational programs or are hired directly to a desk. Rotations can last anywhere from a month to a year, and are designed to both educate new MBAs on various desks and to ensure a good fit prior to placement. New MBAs begin at about $80,000 with a $15,000 mid-year bonus at major Wall Street banks. Second-year associate compensation also tracks closely to that of the second-year corporate finance associate. Associates move to full-fledged trading positions generally in about two to three years, but can move more quickly if they perform well and there are openings (turnover) on the desk.

Full-fledged trading positions

Block traders. These are the folks you see sitting on a desk with dozens of phone lines ringing simultaneously and four or more computer monitors blinking, with orders coming in like machine-gun fire. Typically, traders deal in active, mature markets, such as government securities, stocks, currencies and corporate bonds. Sometimes hailing from top MBA schools, and sometimes tough guys named Vinny from the mailroom, traders historically are hired based on work ethic, attitude and street-smarts.

Sales-traders. A hybrid between sales and trading, sales-traders essentially operate in a dual role as both salesperson and block trader. While block traders deal with huge trades and often massive inventories of stocks or bonds, sales-traders act somewhat as a go-between for salespeople and block traders and trade somewhat smaller blocks of securities. Different from the pure block trader, the sales-trader actually initiates calls to clients, pitches investment ideas and gives market commentary. The sales-trader keeps abreast of market conditions and research commentaries, but, unlike the salesperson, does not need to know the ins and outs of every company when pitching products to clients. Salespeople must be thoroughly versed in the companies they are pitching to clients, whereas sales-traders typically cover the highlights and the big picture. When specific questions arise, a sales-trader will often refer a client to the research analyst.

Structured product traders. At some of the biggest Wall Street firms, structured product traders deal with derivatives, a.k.a. structured products. (**Derivatives** are complex securities that derive their value out of, or have their value contingent on, the values of other assets like stocks, bonds, commodity prices, or market index values.) Because of their complexity, derivatives typically require substantial time to price and structure, so foster an entirely different environment than that of a block trader who deals with heavy trading flows and intense on-the-spot pressure. Note, however, that common stock options (calls and puts) and even Treasury options trade much like any other liquid security. The pricing is fairly transparent, the securities standardized and the volume high. Low-volume, complex derivatives such as interest rate swaps, structured repurchase agreements, and credit derivatives require pricing and typically more legwork prior to trading.

Note that in Trading, job titles can range from Associate to VP to Managing Director. But, the roles as a trader change little. The difference is that MDs typically manage the desks, spending their time dealing with desk issues, risk management issues, personnel issues, etc.

Trader's Compensation: The Bonus Pool

In trading, most firms pay a fixed salary plus a bonus based on the profits the trader brings to the group. Once associates have moved into full-fledged trading roles after two or three years, they begin to be judged by their profit contributions. How much can a trader make? Typically, each desk on the trading floor has a P&L statement for the group. As the group does well, so do the primary contributors. In a down year, everyone suffers. In up years, everyone is happy.

Exactly how the bonuses are determined can be a mystery. Office politics, profits brought into the firm, and tenure all contribute to the final distribution. Often, the MDs on the desk or the top two or three traders on the desk get together and hash out how the bonus pool will be allocated to each person. Then, each trader is told what his or her bonus is. If he or she is unhappy, it is not uncommon for traders (as well as any other employee at an I-bank) to jump ship and leave the firm the second that his or her bonus check clears the bank. Top traders can pull in well over $1 million per year.

Trading — The Routine

The compressed day

Instead of working long hours, traders pack more work into an abbreviated day — a sprint instead of the slow marathon that corporate finance bankers endure. Stress, caffeine, and adrenaline keep traders wired to the markets, their screens, and the trades they are developing. While traders typically arrive by 7 a.m., it is not unheard of to make phone calls to overseas markets in the middle of the night or wake up at 4 a.m. to check on the latest market news from Asia. The link among markets worldwide has never been so apparent as in the past several years, and traders, perhaps more so than any other finance

Visit **Vault Europe's Finance Career Channel** at www.Vault.com/Europe for insider firm profiles, employee surveys of banking profesionals in Europe, job listings, expert finance career advice, insider salary information and more.

VAULT C A R E E R
L I B R A R Y

95

professional, must take care to know the implications of a wide variety of global economic and market events.

Traders consider themselves smarter than the salespeople, who they believe don't understand the products they sell, and bankers, who they believe are slaves with no lives whatsoever. Traders take pride in having free weekends and the option of leaving early on a Friday afternoon. Typically, a trader's day tracks closely to those of the market, and includes an additional two or more hours. Many traders wonder why anyone would become a banker when traders earn as much money with fewer hours.

A London trader's morning usually starts between 6:30 a.m. and 7 a.m., and the day ends soon after the market closes between 5:00 and 5:30 p.m.

Traders typically start the day by checking news, reviewing markets that trade overnight (i.e., Asian markets), and examining their inventory. Typically, at 7:15 a.m., the morning meeting is held to cover a multitude of issues (see inset).

After the morning meeting, between 7:15 and 7:30 a.m., the traders begin to gear up for the market opening. At 8:00 a.m., the fun begins in many fixed income markets — calls begin pouring in and trades start flying. At 8:00 a.m. GMT the London Stock Exchange opens and a flurry of activity immediately ensues.

The Morning Meeting

Every morning of every trading day, each I-banking firm (both in the City and on Wall Street) holds a morning meeting. What happens at these meetings? Besides coffee all around and a few yawns, morning meetings generally are a way to brief sales, trading and research on market activity — past and expected.

At smaller regional firms, the entire equity group usually meets: the salesforce, traders, and research analysts. The bigger firms, because of their sheer size, wire speakers to an overhead speaking system, which is broadcast to the entire equity trading floor. Institutional salespeople and brokers outside the home office also call in to listen in on the meeting.

In fixed income, meetings are often broken down by groups. For example, the government desk, the mortgage desk, the emerging markets desk, and the high yield desk will each have their own morning meetings with the relevant traders, salespeople and research analysts present.

Let's take a look at the participants in morning meetings and their roles:

- In equity, the research analysts review updates to their stocks, present new research and generally discuss the scoop on their universe of stocks. Rating changes and initiation of coverage reports command the most attention to both traders and salespeople on the equity side. In fixed income, meetings will often have analysts who cover economic issues discuss interest rates, Fed activity or market issues, as these often dominate activity in the debt markets.

- Traders cover their inventory, mainly for the benefit of salespeople and brokers in the field. Sometimes a trader eager to move some stock or bonds he or she has carried on the books too long will give quick selling points and indicate where he or she is willing to sell the securities.

- Salespeople, including both brokers and institutional sales, primarily listen and ask relevant questions to the research analyst or to traders, sometimes chipping in with additional information about news or market data.

Morning meetings include rapid-fire discussions on market movements, positions, and trade ideas relevant to them. Time is short, however, so a babbling research analyst will quickly lose the attentions spans of impatient salespeople.

Corporate finance professionals rarely attend morning meetings, choosing instead to show up for work around 9 or 10 a.m.

The day continues with a barrage of market news from the outside, rating changes from research analysts and phone calls from clients. The first breather does not come until lunchtime, when traders take five to grab a sandwich and relax for a few brief minutes. However, the market does not close at lunch, and if a trade is in progress, the traders go without their meals or with meals swallowed at their desks amidst the frenzy. Traders often send an intern to a nearby McDonald's to bring back burgers for the traders.

The action heats up again after lunchtime and continues as before. At 4 p.m., the stock markets officially close and wrap-up begins. Most traders tend to leave around 5 p.m. after closing the books for the day and tying up loose ends. On Fridays, most trading floors are completely empty by 5. Unlike for bankers, for salespeople and traders, golf games, trips to the bar and other social activities are not usually hampered by Friday nights often spent at work.

Visit **Vault Europe's Finance Career Channel** at www.Vault.com/Europe for insider firm profiles, employee surveys of banking profesionals in Europe, job listings, expert finance career advice, insider salary information and more.

VAULT   CAREER LIBRARY   97

A Day in the Life of a Sales-Trader (Lehman Brothers)

Here's a look at a day in the life of a sales-trader, given to us by an associate in the Equities division at Lehman Brothers.

6:30 Get into work. Check voicemail and e-mail. Chat with some people at your desk about the headlines in the *FT,* on Reuters or Bloomberg.

7:15 Equities morning call. You find out what's up to sell. ("I'm sort of a liaison between the accounts [clients] and the block traders. What I do is help traders execute their trading strategies, give them market colour. If they want something I try to find the other side of the trade. Or if I have stuff available, I get info out, without exposing what we have.")

8:00 Markets open. You hit the phones. ("You want to make outgoing calls, you don't really want people to call you. I'm calling my clients, telling them what research is relevant to them, and what merchandise I have, if there's any news on any of their positions.")

10:00 More calls. ("I usually have about 35 different clients. It's always listed equities, but it's a huge range of equities. The client can be a buyer or seller — there's one sales-trader representing a buyer, another representing the seller.")

10:30 On the phone with another Lehman trader, trying to satisfy a client. ("If they have questions in another product, I'll try to help them out.")

11:00 Calling another client. ("It's a trader at the other end, receiving discussions from portfolio manager; their discretion varies from client to client.")

12:00 You hear a call for the sale for a stock that several of your clients are keen on acquiring. ("It's usually a block trader, although sometimes it's another sales-trader. The announcement comes 'over the top,' — over the speaker. It also comes on my computer.")

12:30 Food from the sandwich shop comes in. (You can't go to the bathroom sometimes, say you're working 10 orders, you want to see every stock. We don't leave to get our lunch, we order lunch in.")

1:00 Watching your terminal ("There's a lot of action. If there's 200,000 shares trade in your name [a stock that a client has a position in or

	wants] and it's not you, you want to go back to your client and say who it was.)
2:00	Taking a call from a client. ("You can't miss a beat, you are literally in your seat all day.")
2:05	You tell the client that you have some shares he had indicated interest in previously, but you don't let him know how much you can unload. ("It's a lot of how to get a trade done without disclosing anything that's going to hurt the account. If you have to unload shares you don't want the whole Street to know, or it'll drive down the price.")
5:00	Head home to rest a bit before going out. ("I leave at 5:00 or sometimes 5:30. It depends.")
7:00	Meet a buy-side trader, one of your clients, at a bar. ("We entertain a lot of buy-side traders — dinner, we go to baseball games, we go to bars. Maybe this happens once or twice a week.")

Success factors in trading

There are many keys to success in trading. On the fixed income side, numbers and quantitative skills are especially important, but truly are a prerequisite to survival more than a factor to success. In equities, traders must not only juggle the numbers, but also understand what drives stock prices. These factors include earnings, management assessments, how news affects stocks, etc.

To be one of the best traders, an instinct about the market is key. Some traders look at technical indicators and numbers until they are blue in the face, but without a gut feel on how the market moves, they will never rank among the best. A trader must make rapid decisions at times with little information to go on, and so must be able to quickly assess investor sentiment, market dynamics and the ins and outs of the securities they are trading.

Visit **Vault Europe's Finance Career Channel** at **www.Vault.com/Europe** for insider firm profiles, employee surveys of banking profesionals in Europe, job listings, expert finance career advice, insider salary information and more.

VAULT CAREER LIBRARY 99

Institutional Sales — The Basics

Sales is a core area of any investment bank, comprising the vast majority of people and the relationships that account for a substantial portion of any investment banks' revenues. This section illustrates the divisions seen in sales today at most investment banks. Note, however, that many firms, such as Goldman Sachs, identify themselves as institutionally focused I-banks, and do not even have a retail sales distribution network. Goldman, does, however maintain a solid presence in providing brokerage services to the vastly rich in a division called Private Client Services (PCS for short).

Retail Brokers

Some firms call them account executives and some call them financial advisors or financial consultants. Regardless of this official designator, they are still referring to your classic **retail broker**. The broker's job involves managing the account portfolios for individual investors — usually called retail investors. Brokers charge a commission on any stock trade and also give advice to their clients regarding stocks to buy or sell, and when to buy or sell them. To get into the business, retail brokers must have an undergraduate degree and demonstrated sales skills. Passing the Series 7 and Series 63 examinations are also required before selling commences. Being networked to people with money offers a tremendous advantage for a starting broker.

Institutional Sales

Basically a retail broker with an MBA and more market savvy, the **institutional salesperson** manages the bank's relationships with institutional money managers such as mutual funds or pension funds. Institutional sales is often called research sales, as salespeople focus on selling the firm's research to institutions. As in other areas in banking, the typical hire hails from a top business school and carries a tiptop résumé (that usually involves prior sales experience).

Private Client Services (PCS)

A cross between institutional sales and retail brokerage, **PCS** focuses on providing money management services to extremely wealthy individuals. A client with more than $3 to $5 million in assets usually upgrades from having a classic retail broker deal with him or her to a PCS representative. Similar to institutional sales, PCS generally hires only MBAs with solid selling experience and top credentials. Because PCS representatives become high-end relationship managers, as well as money managers and advisors, the job requires greater expertise than the classic retail broker. Also, because PCS clients trade in larger volumes, the fees and commissions are larger and the number of candidates lining up to become PCS reps is longer.

Institutional Sales – The Players

The players in sales

For many, institutional sales offers the best of all worlds: great pay, fewer hours than in corporate finance or research, less stress than in trading, and a nice blend of travel and office work. Like traders, the hours typically follow the market, with a few tacked on at the end of the day after the market closes. Another plus for talented salespeople is that they develop relationships with key money managers. On the downside, many institutional salespeople complain that many buy-siders disregard their calls, that compensation can exhibit volatile mood swings, that they are overeducated for what they do, and that constantly entertaining clients can prove exhausting.

Sales assistants: This position is most often a dead-end job. It is extremely difficult to move into institutional sales without an MBA, so sales assistants take on a primarily clerical role on the desk. Handling the phones, administrative duties, message taking, letter writing — there's nothing glamorous for the assistants.

Associates: The newly hired MBA is called an associate, or sales associate. Like analogous associates in other investment banking departments, a sales associate spends a year or so in the role learning the ropes and establishing himself. Associates typically spend one to two months rotating through various desks and ensuring a solid fit between the desk and the new associate. Once the rotations end, the associate is placed on a desk and the business of building client relationships begins.

A sales associate joining a leading firm in the City might expect to pull in a base salary of around £45,000, plus a bonus of perhaps £15,000 in the first six months. Pay escalation in the first year depends on the bonus, which often ranges from 50 percent of salary to 90 percent of salary. Beyond that, compensation packages depend on the firm — most firms pay based on commissions generated for the firm.

Salesperson: The associate moves into a full-fledged salesperson role extremely quickly. Within a few months on a desk, the associate begins to handle "B" accounts and gradually

Visit **Vault Europe's Finance Career Channel** at **www.Vault.com/Europe** for insider firm profiles, employee surveys of banking profesionals in Europe, job listings, expert finance career advice, insider salary information and more.

V/\ULT C A R E E R
L I B R A R Y

101

manages them exclusively. A salesperson's ultimate goal is the account at a huge money manager, such as Fidelity or Putnam, that trades in huge volumes on a daily basis. Therefore, a salesperson slowly moves up the account chain, yielding B accounts to younger salespeople and taking on bigger and better "A" accounts. Good salespeople make anywhere from £150,000 to beyond £500,000 and more per year in total compensation.

Salespeople usually focus by region. For example, an institutional equity salesperson will cover all of the buy-side firms in one small region of the country like New England, San Francisco or Chicago. Many salespeople cover New York, as the sheer number of money managers in the City makes for a tremendous volume of work. Salespeople work on specific desks on the trading floor next to traders. Because so much of their work overlaps, sales and trading truly go hand-in-hand. Here's a look at how a trade works from the sales perspective.

The Flow of the Trade: The Sales Perspective

The salesperson has a relationship with a money manager, or an account, as they say. Suppose a research analyst initiates coverage of a new stock with a Buy-1 rating. The salesperson calls the portfolio manager (PM) at the account and gives an overview of the stock and why it is a good buy. The PM will have his own internal research analysts compile a financial model, just as the sell-side research analyst has done, but likely with slightly different expectations and numbers. If the portfolio manager likes the stock, she will contact her trader to work with the trader at the investment bank.

Sell-side research analyst initiates Buy-1 coverage of stock XYZ

▼

Institutional salesperson listens to analyst present stock at morning meeting.

▼

Institutional salesperson understands key points of stock XYZ and calls the portfolio manager (PM) at the buy-side firm.

▼

Salesperson pitches stock to PM.

▼

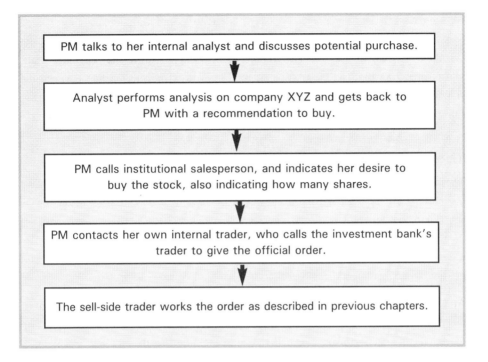

PM talks to her internal analyst and discusses potential purchase.

Analyst performs analysis on company XYZ and gets back to PM with a recommendation to buy.

PM calls institutional salesperson, and indicates her desire to buy the stock, also indicating how many shares.

PM contacts her own internal trader, who calls the investment bank's trader to give the official order.

The sell-side trader works the order as described in previous chapters.

Involvement in an IPO

Corporate finance investment bankers would argue that the salesforce does the least work on an IPO and makes the most money. Salespeople, however, truly help place the offering with various money managers. To give you a breakdown, IPOs typically cost the company going public 7 percent of the gross proceeds raised in the offering. That 7 percent is divided between sales, syndicate and investment banking (i.e., corporate finance) in approximately the following manner:

- 60 percent to Sales
- 20 percent to Corporate Finance
- 20 percent to Syndicate

(If there are any deal expenses, those get charged to the syndicate account and the profits left over from syndicate get split between the syndicate group and the corporate finance group.)

As we can see from this breakdown, the sales department stands the most to gain from an IPO. Their involvement does not begin, however, until a week or two prior to the roadshow. At that point, salespeople begin brushing up on the offering company, making

Visit **Vault Europe's Finance Career Channel** at **www.Vault.com/Europe** for insider firm profiles, employee surveys of banking profesionals in Europe, job listings, expert finance career advice, insider salary information and more.

V/\ULT   CAREER LIBRARY   **103**

calls to their accounts, and pitching the deal. Ideally, they are setting up meetings (called one-on-ones when the meetings are private) between the portfolio manager and the management team of the company issuing the offering. During the roadshow itself, salespeople from the lead underwriter often fly out to attend the meeting between the company and the buy-side PM. While their role is limited during the actual meeting, salespeople essentially hold the PMs' hands, convincing them to buy into the offering.

The sales routine

The institutional salesperson's day begins early. Most arrive at 7 a.m. having already read the morning papers. Each day a package of research is delivered to the salesperson's chair, so reading and skimming these reports begins immediately. The morning meeting at 7:30 involves research commentaries and new developments from research analysts. The trading meeting usually begins 20 minutes later, with updates on trading positions and possible bargains for salespeople to pitch.

At 8 a.m., the salesperson picks up the phone. Calls initially go to the most important of clients, or the bigger clients wishing to get a market overview before trading begins. As the market approaches the opening bell, the salesperson finishes the morning calls and gets ready for the market opening. Some morning calls involve buy or sell ideas, while others involve market updates and stock expectations. At 9:30, the markets open for business, and salespeople continue to call clients, scrutinize the market, and especially look for trading ideas throughout the day.

Day in the Life of a Sales Associate (Bear Stearns)

Here's a look at a day in the life of a sales associate in the Fixed Income division at Bear Stearns in New York.

6:45   Get to work. ("I try to get in around 6:45. Sometimes it's 7:00.)

6:50   After checking e-mail and voice mail, start looking over The Wall Street Journal. ("I get most of my sales ideas from The Wall Street Journal. I'd say 70 to 75 percent of my ideas. I also read the Economist, Business Week, just for an overview, some Barron's and the Financial Times. Maybe three issues out of the five for the week for FT.")

7:15	Start checking Bloombergs, getting warmed up, going over your ideas and figuring out where things stand.
7:45	Meet with your group in a conference room for a brief meeting to go over stuff. ("We go over the traders' axe [what the traders will focus on that day], go over research, what the market quotes are on a particular issue.")
8:15	Get back to desk, and get ready to start pitching ideas.
9:15	Have a short meeting with your smaller group.
10:00	One of your clients calls to ask about bonds from a particular company. You tell her you'll get right back to her. Walk over to talk to an analyst who covers that company. ("I'm in contact a lot with my analyst. I listen to my analyst.")
10:15	Back on the horn with your client.
12:30	Run out to lunch with another salesperson from your group. ("We often buy each other lunch. Sometimes to celebrate a big deal we'll order in lunch. We usually go to Little Italy Pizza Place, or Cosi's Sandwiches. It's always the same people, and it's always the same six places.")
1:00	Back at your desk, check voice mail. ("If I leave for 30 minutes or so, when I get back, I'll have five messages.)
2:00	One of your clients wants to make a move. ("I trade something every day. Maybe anywhere from one to 10 trades. It's on a rolling basis. You plant seeds, and maybe someday one of them grows into a trade.")
3:15	Another client calls and wants to place an order.
5:30	Still on the phone. ("Although the markets close, that's when you can really take the time to talk about where things are and why you think someone should do something.")
7:30	Head for home, you're meeting a client for a late dinner. ("Often on Thursdays we go out as a group.")

Lunchtime is less critical to the salesperson than the trader, although most tend to eat at their desk on the floor. The afternoon often involves more contacting buy-siders regarding trade ideas, as new updates arrive by the minute from research.

isit **Vault Europe's Finance Career Channel** at www.Vault.com/Europe for insider firm
rofiles, employee surveys of banking profesionals in Europe, job listings, expert finance
areer advice, insider salary information and more.

VAULT CAREER LIBRARY 105

The regular session of the major markets close abruptly after 4:00 p.m. By 4:01, many salespeople have fled the building, although many put in a couple more hours of work. Salespeople often entertain buy-side clients in the evening with ball games, fancy dinners, etc.

Success factors in institutional sales

Early on, new associates must demonstrate an ability to get along with the clients they are asked to handle. Usually, the first-year sales associate plays second string to the senior salesperson's account. Any perception that the young salesperson does not get along with the PM or buy-side analyst means he or she may be immediately yanked from the account. Personality, the ability to learn quickly and fit into the sales group will ensure movement up the ladder. The timing of the career path in sales, more so than in corporate finance, depends on the firm. Some firms trust sales associates quickly with accounts, relying on a sink-or-swim culture. Others, especially the biggest I-banks, wait until they are absolutely sure that the sales associate knows the account and what is going on, before handing over accounts.

Once the level of full-on salesperson is reached (usually after one year to one-and-a-half years on the desk), the goal shifts to growing accounts and successfully managing relationships. Developing and managing the relationships at the various buy-side firms is especially critical. Buy-siders can be thought of as time-constrained, wary investors who follow a regimented investing philosophy. Importantly, salespeople must know how and when to contact the investor. For example, a portfolio manager with a goal of finding growth technology stocks will cringe every time a salesperson calls with anything outside of that focused area. Therefore, the salesperson carefully funnels only the most relevant information to the client.

Promotions depend on a combination of individual performance and desk performance. The ability to handle relationships, to bring in new clients, and to generate commission sales for the firm are paramount. Those that have managed to join the ranks of institutional sales without an MBA may be at a disadvantage when it comes to promotions into management roles.

Private Client Services (PCS)

The private client services (PCS) job can be exhilarating, exhausting and frustrating — all at once. As a PCS representative, your job is to bring in individual accounts with at least $2 to $3 million in assets. This involves incessantly pounding the pavement and reading the tape (market news) to find clients, followed by advising them on how to manage their wealth. PCS is a highly entrepreneurial environment. Building the book is all that matters, and managers don't care how a PCS representative spends his or her time, whether this be on the road, in the office, or at parties — the goal is to bring in the cash. Culture-wise, therefore, one typically finds a spirited entrepreneurial group of people, working their own hours and talking on the phone for the better part of the day. It is not uncommon for PCS pros to leave the office early on Fridays with a golf bag slung over one shoulder for a game with existing clients or with a few bigshots with money to invest (read: potential clients).

The growth in PCS

Just a few years ago, PCS was considered a small, unimportant aspect of investment banking. PCS guys were essentially brokers, always bothering other departments for leads and not as sophisticated as their counterparts in corporate finance or institutional sales and trading. Times have changed, however. Today, spurred by the tremendous stock market wealth that has been created over the past few years, PCS is a rapidly growing part of virtually every investment bank. While in the past, many banks essentially had no PCS division, or simply hired a few star retail brokers to be PCS representatives, Wall Street is recruiting heavily on MBA campuses today, scouring to find good talent for PCS.

Getting in the door

It takes an MBA these days, or a stellar record as a retail broker to become a private client sales representative. Even firms such as Merrill Lynch, which historically promoted retail brokers to the PCS role, are moving more and more toward hiring only those with business degrees from top schools and proven selling credentials, rather than proven brokers. PCS is also evolving into an entirely different business from traditional retail brokerage.

Whereas retail brokers make money on commissions generated through trades, PCS reps are increasingly charging clients just as money managers do — as a percentage of assets under management. A typical fee might be 1 percent per year of total assets under management. This fee obviously increases as the value of the assets increases, thereby motivating the PCS worker to generate solid returns on the portfolio. This move to fee-

isit **Vault Europe's Finance Career Channel** at **www.Vault.com/Europe** for insider firm
ofiles, employee surveys of banking profesionals in Europe, job listings, expert finance
areer advice, insider salary information and more.

V∧ULT   CAREER
LIBRARY   **107**

based management is designed to take away the incentive of a salesperson to churn or trade an account just for the sake of the commissions. One should note, however, that the trend to charge a fee instead of commissions is just that — a trend. Many Wall Street PCS reps still work on a commission basis.

The associate position

Once in the door, as a PCS associate, extensive training begins. The PCS associate must be well versed in all areas of the market and able to understand a wide variety of investing strategies. While a corporate bond salesperson has to know only corporate bonds, a PCS rep must be able to discuss the big picture of the market, equities, bonds, and even a slew of derivative products. Thus, training is said to be intensive in PCS, with many weeks of classroom learning.

Once training is complete, a new PCS associate often works to find his way onto a team, which pairs PCS beginners with one or two experienced PCS reps. (Teams are the latest craze on Wall Street.) The process of matching a new associate onto a team is driven largely by personality and fit. Once paired with an older rep or two, the associate works to understand the process of finding new clients and managing a portfolio of assets.

Generally speaking, PCS hires are given two years to build a book, or establish a reasonable level of business for the firm. While salaries for PCS associates out of business school matches those of other City hires (about £68,000 plus a stub bonus in the first six months), they quickly are shifted to a straight commission basis.

How to Build a Book

PCS associates must establish themselves in the first two years through any means possible. Typically, once the PCS associate has learned how to pitch to clients and how to give money-management advice, he or she begins to look for leads. As PCS is a sales job, leads and clients are developed just like at any other sales job. Phone calls, networking and visiting potential clients are key. To find leads, associates might do any of the following:

• Read the tape (follow market news). Many news articles in the markets discuss companies merging, companies going public, companies selling out, management selling stock in their companies, etc. In these cases, there often are CEOs and others on the management team who will find themselves with gobs of cash that must be invested. These are excellent sources of leads.

- Follow up with leads from other areas within the investment bank. A substantial number of corporate finance bankers represent management teams selling stock in public offerings, or selling stock in mergers. The real bonus is that the bankers already know the CEO or CFO with newfound wealth, and can provide an excellent introduction.

- Network. The power of being a friend of a friend cannot be underestimated. That is why PCS reps spend time at parties, functions, on the golf course, and anywhere else they can find leads. Often an "in" such as an introduction provided by a personal friend is the best lead of all.

Pay beyond the associate level

After a successful client list has been established, the sky is the limit in terms of pay. The best of the best PCS pros can earn well over £500,000 a year. The bottom-of-the-barrel PCS reps, however, may take home a mere £100,000 or so. The average number is somewhere around £250,00 for a PCS pro working for a leading City firm. Insiders say it takes an average of five or six years to reach that level, however. Still, there are exceptions. One insider at Goldman Sachs reports that a PCS representative with that firm reached $3.4 million in compensation only five years out of business school.

Managing the portfolio

You may wonder how a PCS representative with a substantial client base and millions of dollars under account manages all these assets. It actually depends on the firm. Some firms break the PCS job into relationship managers and portfolio managers. For example, at JPMorgan, some PCS reps solely manage the portfolios of the various accounts, and are even paid a straight salary and bonus, depending on returns, while other reps work on client relations. Other firms, with newly built or bought asset management divisions, are attempting to pair PCS and AM (asset management) in order to utilize the existing money management expertise. Goldman Sachs, for example, has sought to do this, but cultural differences between the divisions and the past ingrained modus operandi may be a hindrance. Regardless of how the portfolio is managed, the movement toward teams will

sit **Vault Europe's Finance Career Channel** at www.Vault.com/Europe for insider firm ofiles, employee surveys of banking profesionals in Europe, job listings, expert finance reer advice, insider salary information and more.

V/\ULT C A R E E R
L I B R A R Y   **109**

be a key to melding asset management and relationship management expertise in the City or on Wall Street.

Key success factors in PCS

One should keep in mind that PCS divisions essentially want to hire good salespeople, not good number crunchers. They don't need or want quant jocks in PCS; they want salespeople and schmoozers to find and land new clients. The key to succeeding in PCS is generating more assets to manage.

Good PCS reps will manage their client relationships extremely well, as these clients become the bread and butter for them over time. Understanding the goals of clients and executing them are extremely important. For example, one finds in PCS that some investors are not out to beat the S&P at all, and would rather earn steady returns without risking their principal. Remember, a wealthy and retired ex-CEO may not care that his $50 million jackpot beats the market. After all, he's got much more than he could spend in a lifetime. Lower risk and decent returns work just fine in some cases, and PCS representatives must be attuned to these individual differences.

Research

If you have a brokerage account, you have likely been given access to research on stocks that you asked about. This research was probably written by an investment banks' research department.

To the outsider, it seems that research analysts spend their time in a quiet room poring over numbers, calling companies, and writing research reports. The truth is an entirely different story, involving quite a bit of selling on the phone and on the road. Analysts produce research ideas, hand them to associates and assistants, and then man the phone talking to buy-side stock/bond pickers, company managers, and internal salespeople. They become the managers of research reports and the experts on their industries to the outside world. Thus, while the lifestyle of the research analyst would initially appear to resemble that of a statistician, it often comes closer to that of a diplomat or salesperson.

The Players

Research assistants

The bottom-level number crunchers in research, research assistants generally begin with no industry or market expertise. They come from solid undergraduate schools and performed well in school, but initially perform mundane research tasks, such as digging up information and editing/formatting reports. Research assistants also take over the spreadsheet modeling functions required by the analyst. Travel is limited for the budding research assistant, as it usually does not make sense financially to send more than the research analyst to meetings with company officials or money managers.

Research associates

Burdened with numbers and deadlines, the research associate often feels like a cross between a statistician and a corporate finance analyst. Long hours, weekends in the office and number-crunching sum up the routine of the associate. However, compared to analyst and associate analogues in corporate finance, the research associate works fewer hours, often makes it home at a reasonable time, and works less on the weekend. Unfortunately, the associate is required to be present and accounted for at 7:30 a.m., when most morning meetings take place.

Mirroring the corporate finance analyst and associate positions, research associates can be bright, motivated kids directly out of top undergraduate universities, or at firms dedicated to hiring MBAs in research, the research associate role is the entry-level position once the MBA has been earned.

A talented research associate can earn much in the way of responsibility. For example, the research associate may field phone calls from smaller "B" accounts (i.e., smaller money managers) and companies less important to the analyst. (The analyst handles the relationships with the biggest buy-siders, best clients and top salespeople.) When it comes to writing reports, some analysts give free reign to associates in writing. Also, research associates focus on one industry and typically work for only one full-fledged research analyst. This structure helps research associates delve deeper into the aspects of one industry group and enable them to work closely with a senior-level research analyst.

To start, research assistants/associates out of undergraduate typically get paid similarly to the corporate finance analyst right out of college. After one or two years, the compensation varies dramatically, depending on performance and the success of the analysts in the industry group as well as the associate's contribution. For the MBA research associate, the compensation is similar to I-banking associates: around £50,000 salaries with perhaps a £15,000 signing bonus, plus maybe a £15,000 year-end bonus.

It All Depends on the Analyst

Insiders stress that the research associate's contribution entirely depends on the particular analyst. Good analysts (from the perspective of the associate) encourage responsibility and hand-off a significant amount of work. Others communicate poorly, maintain rigid control and don't trust their assistants and associates to do much more than the most mundane tasks.

Being stuck with a mediocre analyst can make your job miserable. If you are considering an entry-level position in research, you should carefully evaluate the research analyst you will work with, as this person will have a huge impact on your job experience.

Note that in research, the job titles for analyst and associate have switched. In corporate finance, one begins as an analyst, and is promoted to associate post-MBA. In research, one begins as a research associate, and ultimately is promoted to the research analyst title.

Research analysts

The research analyst, especially in equity, is truly a guru. Analysts follow particular industries, recommend stocks to buy and sell, and convince salespeople and buy-siders why they or their clients should or should not invest in Company XYZ. The road to becoming an analyst is either paved with solid industry experience, or through the research assistant/associate path.

Full-fledged analyst positions are difficult to come by. The skills required to succeed as an analyst include a firm grasp of: 1) the industry and dynamics of stock picking, and 2) the sales skills required to convince investors and insiders alike why a stock is such an excellent buy. An analyst lacking in either area will simply not become the next *II*-rated star (that is, an analyst highly rated by the annual *Institutional Investor* poll).

Research analysts spend considerable time talking on the phone to investors, salespeople and traders, pitching buy and sell ideas or simply discussing industry or company trends. Everyone tries to get the research analyst's ear, to ask for advice or (as we will discuss in-depth later) to pressure him or her to change a rating or initiate coverage of a particular stock. Analysts also travel regularly, visiting buy-siders or big money managers and companies in their field. Indirectly, they are trying to generate trading business with money managers, research ideas from companies or trying to build a reputation in the industry. All in all, analysts must be able to convincingly and quickly pitch an idea, and defend it thoroughly when the time comes.

In this atmosphere, research analysts must scrutinize every company that they maintain under coverage. Any news or company announcements will spur a deluge of phone calls to the analyst, with questions ranging from the big picture to the tiniest of details. They also must maintain a handle on an extremely important aspect of any company — the numbers. Inaccurate earnings estimates, especially when they are far from the mark, reflect poorly on the analyst. Why didn't an analyst know the company stock was going to come out with such low earnings? Or, why didn't the research analyst know that industry growth was slowing down? The analyst is responsible for staying on top of these things.

Compensation packages for research analysts run the gamut. Some *II*-rated star analysts in hot industries command multimillion dollar annual packages, especially during bull markets. Most banks figure their compensation for analysts with formulas that are usually incomprehensible to even the research analysts. The factors that go into analyst compensation typically includes a mix of the following:

sit **Vault Europe's Finance Career Channel** at www.Vault.com/Europe for insider firm ofiles, employee surveys of banking profesionals in Europe, job listings, expert finance reer advice, insider salary information and more.

V/\ULT CAREER LIBRARY 113

- The performance of stocks under coverage (meaning that if their stocks perform like the analyst predicts, they get paid well)

- Trading activity within the firm of stocks under coverage

- Corporate finance business revenues of companies in their industry

- Performance evaluations of the research analyst by superiors

- *Institutional Investor* rankings (Once a research analyst finds himself listed as an *II*-ranked analyst, the first stop is into his boss's office to renegotiate his annual package.)

Note: As they progress in their career, research analysts receive titles similar to investment bankers, namely VP, SVP and ultimately MD. However, the tasks of a research analyst tend to remain somewhat consistent once the analyst level is reached, with perhaps more selling of research and traveling involved at the most senior levels, and more oversight of a group of more junior analysts.

The Institutional Investor (II)
Ratings Scorecard

Institutional Investor is a monthly magazine publication that, among other things, rates research analysts. The importance of the II ratings to investment banks and even many institutional investors cannot be overstated. Most industry watchers believe and follow the ratings as if they were gospel.

How do the ratings work? Essentially, II utilizes a formula to determine the best research analysts on Wall Street, surveys industry professionals, and publishes their rankings annually. Note the bias, however, toward research analysts at bulge bracket firms in these ratings. II's formula essentially involves surveys of "directors of research, chief investment officers, portfolio managers, and buy-side analysts at the major money management institutions around the world." Major money managers deal primarily with large investment banks for their trading needs and a portion of their research needs.

In 2003 Lehman Brothers took the top spot in the II rankings, with 50 analysts rated. Morgan Stanley shot up from No. 5 in 2002 to take the No. 2 spot in 2003 with 36 analysts rated. Merrill placed No. 3 down one notch from its No. 2 finish in 2002. And Citigroup fell from No. 1 to No. 4.

The Product

Industry research reports

To establish oneself as a knowledgeable analyst, many researchers begin by writing and issuing an industry piece. For example, an industry research report on the oil and gas sector might discuss issues such as commodity prices, the general outlook for the sector and valuations of companies in the industry.

The time required to generate an industry piece depends on the length of the report, the complexity of the industry, and how important it is to show expertise to investors and management teams in the industry. For completely new industries for new analysts, a full six months or more is given to enable the analyst to fully understand the industry and develop a thorough report. Once it is printed, salespeople will use an industry research report to get up to speed and learn about a particular segment.

Touted as industry gospel, industry research reports take substantial time to produce and earn the firm nothing except awareness that the investment bank follows an industry and has expertise in that industry. However, the brand equity built by an industry piece can be substantial and make corporate finance banker cold-calling a much easier process.

Company-specific research reports

Once an analyst's industry piece has been written and digested by the investment community, the analyst focuses on publishing research reports on specific companies. To create a well-rounded research universe, research analysts will typically write on the top industry players, as well as several smaller players in the industry. One of the most critical roles of an equity research analyst is to make future earnings estimates for the companies he or she covers. (The average earnings estimate of all analysts covering a company is called the "consensus" estimate.) Company-specific reports fall into three categories: initiation of coverage, updates and rating changes.

Initiation of coverage: This is exactly what it sounds like. These reports indicate that an analyst has not previously written research or covered the particular company. Usually an initiation of coverage report includes substantial information about the business, a detailed forecast model and risk factors inherent in the business.

Update: When a stock moves, news/earnings are released, or the analyst meets with management, an update report is put out. Often one-pagers, updates provide quick

sit **Vault Europe's Finance Career Channel** at www.Vault.com/Europe for insider firm
ofiles, employee surveys of banking profesionals in Europe, job listings, expert finance
reer advice, insider salary information and more.

VAULT CAREER
LIBRARY 115

information important to current movements in the stock or will raise or lower earnings estimates.

Change of rating: Whenever an I-bank alters its rating on a stock (we will discuss these ratings later), a report is issued. These reports vary in length from one to five pages. Reasons for a downgrade include: lower than expected earnings, forecasts for diminished industry or firm growth, management departures, problems integrating a merger, or even overpriced stocks. Reasons for an upgrade include: better than expected earnings, new management, stock repurchases, or beneficial industry trends.

Conflict of Interest

A monumental securities investigation came to end in 2002, forever altering the way investment banks do business. In December 2002, 10 of Wall Street's largest investment firms agreed to pay $1.4 billion to settle research and advisory conflicts-of-interest violations. The settlement closed an investigation that was initially opened by New York State Attorney General Eliot Spitzer, which began in early 2002 with an investigation into research practices at banking behemoth Merrill Lynch. Spitzer alleged that research analysts there allowed potential investment banking fees to influence the ratings given to companies covered by the firm.

Market commentary

Analysts usually cover a particular (small) universe of stocks, but some analysts, called market strategists, survey and report on market conditions as a whole. Most large banks publish market commentary reports on a daily basis (sometimes even several within a day), augmented with weekly, monthly and quarterly reviews. Included in such reports is information on the performance of stocks in major market indices in the U.S., major markets worldwide, and in various sectors — such as transportation, technology and energy — in the U.S. Some of these commentaries offer forecasts for the markets or for particular sectors. Naturally, economic data is paramount to stock market performance overall and thus pervades market commentaries.

Economic commentary

Similar to a market commentary, economic reports are also published periodically and cover economic indicators and trends. These reports are often stuffed with graphs of macroeconomic factors such as GDP, inflation, interest rates, consumer spending, new home sales, import/export data, etc. They provide useful information regarding government fiscal and monetary policy, and often link to fixed income reports. Often the same market strategist writes both the economic commentaries and the market commentaries for a firm.

Fixed income commentary

Analysts covering the fixed income markets publish periodic reports on the debt markets. Often tied to the economic commentaries, fixed income market reports comment on the performance of various fixed income instruments including U.S. government securities, mortgages, corporate bonds, commodity prices and other specialized fixed income securities. The three-point scale for rating stocks has become ubiquitous in banking (since the conflicts-of-interest settlement), but the definitions that banks refer to do not accurately measure what the analyst believes. The following scale reflects the general consensus on stock ratings, but keep in mind that these vary by firm.

Rating	Published Definition	Actual Meaning
Outperform	STRONG BUY. The company's stock is a strong buy, and will outperform the market over the next 18 months.	The stock is a worthy buy. Or, if the investment bank writing the research just completed a transaction for the company, the analyst may simply believe it is a decent company that will perform as well as the market in the next 18 months.
Neutral	MARKET PERFORM. The stock will perform approximately as well as the market over the next 18 months.	Be wary about buying this stock. It is either richly valued or has potential problems which will inhibit the firm's growth over the next 18 months.
Underperfom	SELL. The stock will perform below the market over the next 18 months	Dump this stock as soon as possible. An underperform rating issued by an analyst means the company is not moving in the right direction.

isit **Vault Europe's Finance Career Channel** at **www.Vault.com/Europe** for insider firm rofiles, employee surveys of banking profesionals in Europe, job listings, expert finance areer advice, insider salary information and more.

VAULT CAREER LIBRARY **117**

Three Months in Research

The cycle

Many research analysts comment that there's not a typical day, nor even a typical week in research. On the equity side, the workload is highly cyclical. Everything revolves around earnings reports, which come out quarterly during **earnings season**. The importance of the earnings figures to the stock analyst cannot be stressed enough, and once a quarter, when companies report their earnings data, the job often gets a little crazy.

On the fixed income side, the workflow depends entirely on the product. A high yield or high grade corporate bond research analyst may have some ups and downs in the workload based on the earnings season, but earnings reports are not nearly as critical as they are to equity analysts. We will cover a typical day in debt research in abbreviated form at end of this chapter. First we'll take a look at a three-month period for an equity research analyst.

While we will focus on the analyst himself, keep in mind that the research associate will also perform many of the same tasks, helping the analyst in any way possible.

March

On March 1, four weeks prior to the end of the quarter (March 31), the analyst begins to look at the financial models relating to the companies under coverage. He is worried about his stocks' earnings per share numbers, which will be reported approximately two to four weeks after the quarter's end. If the estimated EPS numbers stray too far from the actual reported EPS when it comes out, the analyst will find himself dealing with many angry investors and salespeople, at the very least.

To finetune his earnings estimates, the analyst begins calling the companies that he covers, testing assumptions, refining certain predictions, and generally trying to grasp exactly where the company and industry stand. Details make the difference, and the analyst discusses with the company CFO gross margin estimates, revenue predictions, and even tax issues, to arrive at an acceptable EPS figure. Conversations such as these can become excruciatingly detailed.

April

The quarter has ended, and in early April the research analyst enters the quiet period. During this time companies are restricted from discussing their upcoming earnings release, as this may constitute sensitive inside information. The calm before the storm, the quiet period (in this case, early April) finds many analysts calling other contacts in the industry to discuss broader trends and recent developments in the field.

Once companies begin reporting earnings (which starts mid-month), the analyst scrambles to quickly digest the information and issue one-page update reports. The deluge of company earnings releases causes long and hectic days for the analyst, who must deal with a barrage of phone calls and the demand for written reports from salespeople and institutional investors. Within two weeks after the earnings release, the analyst will typically publish another three-page report on his companies, often with new ratings, new analysis and revised earnings estimates for the next few quarters.

May

In early May, the analyst finishes writing update reports and is afforded a little breathing room. While earnings season involves putting out fires left and right, the end of the reporting period means the analyst can relax and get back to working on long-term projects. These might include industry pieces, initiation reports or other long-term projects. Banks with large corporate finance businesses may encourage their research analysts and associates to spend time working with investment bankers, developing leads, advising them who to target, and performing a variety of other research tasks.

Travel

You'd better like suitcases and hotel rooms if you're aiming for a research analyst position — the position requires a great deal of travel. Usually, the full-fledged analyst (as opposed to the associate) does most of the work requiring travel, including meeting with money managers (the buy-side clients), company management, accompanying corp fin professionals on roadshows. However, associates will fill in for unavailable analysts, attend some due diligence meetings, and attend conferences and trade shows.

These occasional outside meetings aside, research associates spend almost all of their time in the home office. On the plus side, many associates often meet with managers of the companies that come to visit the bank, meaning research associates have the luxury of meeting one-on-one with top management teams and investor relations representatives. This is especially the case in New York, where research analysts with big firms carry a lot of influence.

sit **Vault Europe's Finance Career Channel** at www.Vault.com/Europe for insider firm
ofiles, employee surveys of banking profesionals in Europe, job listings, expert finance
areer advice, insider salary information and more.

V/\ULT   CAREER
         LIBRARY   **119**

Writing the report

Where do new research ideas come from? And when and why do analysts change their ratings?

Frankly, many young analysts are told what companies or areas to cover — until one becomes a seasoned analyst, an analyst focuses on ideas based on firm demands. Veteran analysts with more leeway generate ideas either through industry knowledge or new stocks. Typically, investment banks will compel an analyst to follow a particular stock but will not dictate the rating assigned to the stock. The pressure to publish certain ratings, however, is real and cannot be understated, as it can come from all angles.

The writing process is straightforward, and really depends on the type of report needed. For the inch-thick industry report, for example, research analysts utilize research associates and assistants to the utmost. Analysts coordinate the direction, thesis, and basic content of the report, and do much of the writing. For an introductory initiation of coverage report, the work parallels the industry piece. Substantial research, financial analysis and information gathering require much time and effort. Behind the scenes, management interviews and company visits to understand and probe the business render the biggest volume of data.

For less labor-intensive pieces, such as changes in ratings or updates, either the analyst or the associate whips out the report in short time. Keep in mind that the analyst usually produces the idea and reviews the report prior to press time, but the associate may in reality put together the entire piece (and put the analyst's name on top).

For all of these reports, research associates and assistants typically find data, compile other research, edit the written material, build financial models and construct graphs and charts of relevant information. The analyst utilizes his or her contacts within the industry to interview insiders to get a glimpse of the latest trends and current events.

Commonly Used Ratios

Solvency Ratios		
Quick Ratio =	Cash + Accts Rec Total Current Liabilities	Shows the dollars of liquid assets (convertible into cash within 30 days) available to cover each dollar of current debt.
Current Ratio =	Total Current Assets Total Current Liabilities	Measures the margin of safety present to cover any possible reduction of current assets.
Current Liabilities to Net Worth =	Total Current Liabilities Net Worth	Contrasts the amounts due creditors within a year with the funds permanently invested by owners. The smaller the net worth and the larger the liabilities, the greater the risk.
Current Liabilities to Inventory =	Total Liabilities Net Worth	Compares the company's total indebtedness to the venture capital invested by the owners. High debt levels can indicate greater risk.
Fixed Assets to Net Worth =	Fixed Assets Net Worth	Reflects the portion of net worth that consists of fixed assets. Generally, a smaller ratio is desired.

Efficiency Ratios		
Collection Period =	Accounts Receivable x 365 Sales	Reflects the average number of days it takes to collect receivables
Inventory Turnover =	Sales Inventory	Determine the rate at which merchandise is being moved and the effect of the flow of funds into a business.
Assets to Sales =	Total Assets Sales	This rate ties in sales and the total investment in assets that is used to generate those sales.
Sales to Net Working Capital =	Sales Net Working Capital*	Measures the efficiency of management to use its short-term assets and liabilities to generate revenues
Accounts Payable to Sales =	Accounts Payable Sales	Measure the extent to which the supplier's money is being used to generate sales. When this ratio is multiplied by 365 days, it reflects the average number of days it takes the company to repay its suppliers.

Probability Ratios		
Return on Sales (Profit Margin) =	Net Profit After Taxes Sales	Reveals profits earned per dollar of sales and measures the efficiency of the operation.
Return on Assets =	Net Profit After Taxes Total Assets	This is the key indicator of profitability for a firm. It matches net profits with the assets available to earn a return.
Return on Net Worth (Return on Equity) =	Net Profit after Taxes Net Worth	Analyzes the ability of the firm's management to realize an adequate return on the capital invested by the owners of the firm.

* Net Working Capital = Current Assets — Current Liabilities
Source: Dun & Bradstreet

Visit **Vault Europe's Finance Career Channel** at **www.Vault.com/Europe** for insider firm profiles, employee surveys of banking profesionals in Europe, job listings, expert finance career advice, insider salary information and more.

VAULT CAREER LIBRARY

121

Fixed income research — yawning?

The attitude of many equity bankers, equity sales and traders, and even some equity research analysts is that fixed income research is the most boring area in any investment bank. Why? Unlike stock analysts, many fixed income analysts do not have clients. If a fixed income analyst issues a report on U.S. Treasury bonds, there is no company calling, fewer surprises, and few salespeople/traders to sing the praises of a good research piece. More importantly, there is often less money to make. While equity analysts often can rise to stardom (i.e., *II* ranking), those that do in fixed income play second fiddle to the equity guys. All in all, the fixed income research job is one of the least glamorous on the Street.

A day in the life of a fixed income analyst

How is the debt analyst different than the equity analyst? As previously mentioned, there is no earnings season driving fixed income as much as there is in equity. But corporate bond analysts and high yield analysts do have some seasonal swings. In municipal bond research, emerging markets research, asset-backed research, and government/Treasury research, reports are more evenly spaced and the stress and pressure often lower. But certain monthly events and surprising news (usually macroeconomic in nature) can spark analysts to stay busy. For example, U.S. Treasury research reports often come out around monthly CPI, PPI and quarterly GDP numbers. In general, interest rate news always impacts bonds, and creates work for analysts to interpret.

The day begins early for the debt research analyst just as it does for the equity analyst. Morning meetings take place around 7:30, no matter where you may happen to work.

The day includes all of the typical work that an equity research analyst does. The analyst is on the phone with buy-side portfolio managers, doing fundamental research, writing reports, tracking bond prices and yield data, and looking for trade ideas to give to the salesforce. Hours tend to resemble the equity analyst, with 12- to 13-hour days the norm, but with less time on the road.

Formulas for Success

Research assistants/associates

To excel initially, research assistants and associates must work hard, learn quickly, and become whizzes at Microsoft Excel and Word. Especially important to research associates are good writing skills, as analysts often hand-off a significant portion of the writing and editing of research reports to the associate. Early on, the biggest mistake a research assistant or associate can make is to mess up the financial models and generally lose sight of the details.

Research is built on a foundation of good models with reasonable assumptions, and research associates must first master that domain. Later on, research assistants and associates must show an ability to handle the phones — answer questions from investors and internal salespeople about the current goings-on at companies they cover, as well as ask smart due diligence questions to company managers in order to generate the next research piece.

Unlike most corporate finance analysts, research assistants/associates can and do rise to the analyst level without an MBA. Some firms promote research assistants to the full-fledged analyst role after one or two years of solid performance, while some hire research associates only for two-year stints, emulating the corporate finance two-year programs. The firms that are less stringent about hiring MBAs full-time for research are more likely to promote internal associates to the analyst position.

Still, the number that makes this jump is a small portion of assistants and associates. Why? Some simply discover that the analyst job is not for them. Many research dropouts move to hedge funds, business school, the buy-side, or institutional sales departments at I-banks. Others simply find that the path to becoming a research analyst nonexistent. Explains one research associate at Morgan Stanley, "A lot of it's demand-driven. If you want to be the head technology analyst, you might have to wait until that person retires or moves to another firm. But sometimes they will add on analysts, maybe they need a retail analyst to bring I-banking business in. And sometimes a new subsector will turn into a new category."

Research analysts

Newly hired research analysts must start as the associates do — learning, modeling, and working long hours. Beyond the inaugural two years, analysts begin to branch out and become full-fledged analysts, covering their own set of stocks and their own industry segment or sub-segment. Winning respect internally from corp fin and sales and trading departments may be the first hurdle a new analyst must overcome. This respect comes from detailed research and careful analysis before making assertions about anything. Salespeople can be ruthless when it comes to researchers who make sloppy or unsubstantiated claims. Says one fixed income insider, "There are people who will eat you alive if your analysis is off. They control a huge universe of issues and a huge amount of buyers to make that market liquid, and when you

Visit **Vault Europe's Finance Career Channel** at www.Vault.com/Europe for insider firm profiles, employee surveys of banking profesionals in Europe, job listings, expert finance career advice, insider salary information and more.

VAULT CAREER LIBRARY **123**

present your analysis you had better be ready. These guys are serious. It's like playing for the San Francisco 49ers; you better be prepared."

Down the road, research analysts — even good ones — are always on somebody's bad side. When the analyst wins respect from the salesperson by turning down a potentially bad IPO, he angers to no end the corporate finance banker who wants to take the company public. When the analyst puts a sell recommendation on a poor stock, the salespeople also cheer, but the company grows angry, sometimes severing all ties with their investment bank. Thus, the best analysts function as diplomats, capable of making clear objective arguments regarding decisions combined with a mix of sweet-talking salespeople and investors.

Do Research Analysts Need MBAs and CFAs?

Although not required, an MBA opens doors in research. Ten years ago, research departments cared little about educational pedigree and a business school education, but today more and more emphasis is being placed on attaining an MBA. On Wall Street, perhaps even more important than earning an MBA for those in research is becoming a **Chartered Financial Analyst**, or CFA. The Association of Investment Management and Research (AIMR) confers this designation on those who pass a series of examinations, which are administered in three stages. They are Levels I, II and III and are given at one-year intervals in May. To become a CFA, one must pass all three levels and also have worked for three years (which usually coincides with the testing period). The program and tests are not easy, and according to the AIMR the pass rates have ranged over the past 10 years:

- Level I: 48 percent to 62 percent
- Level II: 46 percent to 65 percent
- Level III: 59 percent to 82 percent

The CFA designation lends the analyst respect and credibility to investors and seems more and more a prerequisite to moving up. As one analyst notes, "All things being equal, promotions will go to the analyst with his CFA examinations complete or with his MBA degree." In addition, a candidate interviewing for a research position will stand out by stating a sincere intention to complete the CFA examinations.

Syndicate:
The Go-Betweens

What does the syndicate department at an investment bank do? Syndicate usually sits on the trading floor, but syndicate employees don't trade securities or sell them to clients. Neither do they bring in clients for corporate finance.

What syndicate does is provide a vital role in placing stock or bond offerings with buy-siders, and truly aim to find the right offering price that satisfies both the company, the salespeople, the investors and the corporate finance bankers working the deal.

Syndicate and public offerings

In any public offering, syndicate gets involved once the prospectus is filed with the SEC. At that point, syndicate associates begin to contact other investment banks interested in being underwriters in the deal. Before we continue with our discussion of the syndicate's role, we should first understand the difference between managers and underwriters and how fees earned through security offerings are allocated.

Managers

The managers of an IPO get involved from the beginning. These are the I-banks attending all the meetings and generally slaving away to complete the deal. Managers get paid a substantial portion of the total fee — called underwriting discounts and commissions on the cover of a prospectus, and known as the spread in the industry. On Wall Street in an IPO, the spread is usually 7.0 percent, unless the deal is huge, which often means that the offering company can negotiate a slightly lower fee. For a follow-on offering, typical fees start at 5.0 percent, and again, decrease as the deal-size increases.

As discussed previously in this guide, deals typically have between two and five managers. To further confuse the situation, managers are often called managing underwriters, as all managers are underwriters, but not all underwriters are managers. Confused? Keep reading.

Underwriters

The **underwriters** on the deal are so called because they are the ones assuming liability, though they usually have no shares of stock to sell in the deal. They are not necessarily the I-banks that work intimately on the deal; most underwriters do nothing other than accept any potential liability for lawsuits against the underwriting group.

Visit **Vault Europe's Finance Career Channel** at **www.Vault.com/Europe** for insider firm profiles, employee surveys of banking profesionals in Europe, job listings, expert finance career advice, insider salary information and more.

VAULT CAREER LIBRARY 125

Underwriters are selected by the lead manager in conjunction with the company. This role is often called participating in the syndicate. In a prospectus, you can always find a section entitled "Underwriting," which lists the underwriting group. Anywhere from 10 to 30 investment banks typically make up the underwriting group in any securities offering.

In the underwriting section, the list of each participant has next to it listed a number of shares. While underwriting sections list quite a few investment banks and shares next to each bank, it is important to realize that these banks do not sell shares. Neither do they have anything to do with how the shares in the deal are allocated to investors. They merely assume the percentage of liability indicated by the percentage of deal shares listed in the prospectus. To take on such liability, underwriters are paid a small fee, depending on their level of underwriting involvement (i.e., the number of shares next to their name). The managers in the deal will account for the liability of approximately 50 to 70 percent of the shares, while the underwriters account for the rest.

The Economics of a Deal

Suppose there are three managers in an IPO transaction for ABC Corporation. Say the deal is $200 million in size. And let's say that this $200 million is accounted for because the deal is priced at $20 per share and the company is offering 10 million shares to the public. With a 7.0 percent spread (the deal fee percent typical in IPOs), we come up with a whopping $14 million fee.

How is the $14 million divied up? Each department is actually allocated a piece of the deal before the firms divide their shares. First, corporate finance (the bankers working the deal) grabs 20 percent of the fee. So, in our example, $2.8 million (20 percent of $14 million) is split among the three managers' corp fin departments. Then the salespeople from the managing group take their share — a whooping 60 percent of the spread, totaling $8.4 million. Again, this $8.4 million is divided by the few managers in the deal.

This 20/60 split is typical for almost any deal. The last portion of the spread goes to the syndicate group (a.k.a. the underwriters) and is appropriately called the underwriting fee. However, expenses for the deal are taken out of the underwriting fee, so it never amounts to a full 20 percent of the spread. Suppose that this deal had 20 underwriters. The underwriting section in the prospectus might look like:

The total number of shares accounted for by each underwriter (the number of shares each underwriter assumes liability for) adds up to the total number of shares sold in the transaction. Note that the managers or underwriting managers take the biggest chunk of the liability. (In this case, each manager would pay 25 percent of damages from a lawsuit, as 5,000,000 shares represent 25 percent of the 20,000,000-share offering.)

If we return to our example, we see that after the sales and corporate finance managers are paid, the last 20 percent comes out to $2.8 million. This is quite a bit, but remember that the way deals work, expenses are netted against the underwriting fee. Flights to the company, lawyers, roadshow expenses, etc., all add up to a lot of money and are taken out of the underwriting fee. Why? Nobody exactly knows why this is the practice, except that it doesn't seem quite fair to have the syndicate receive as much as the bankers — who put in countless weekends and hours putting together a deal.

Let's pretend that deal expenses totaled $1.8 million, leaving

$2.8 million   Underwriting Fees

- $1.8 million   Expenses

Underwriting Profit $1.0 million

Therefore, the lead manager gets 35 percent of the underwriting profit (7,000,000 shares divided by the total 20,000,000 = 35 percent). The two co-managers each receive 20 percent of the underwriting profit (4,000,000 divided by 20,000,000) and each underwriter receives approximately 1.47 percent of the underwriting profit (294,118 divided by 20,000,000). Therefore the lead manager gets $350,000 of the underwriting profit, the co-managers each get $200,000, and the other underwriters each get approximately $14,706. Not bad for doing practically nothing but taking on minimal risk.

Why the long diversion into the mechanics of what an underwriter is and how much they are paid? Because this is what syndicate spends considerable time doing.

Syndicate professionals:

- Make sure their banks are included in the underwriting of other deals
- Put together the underwriting group in deals the I-bank is managing
- Allocate stock to the various buy-side firms indicating interest in deal
- Determine the final offering price of various offerings

Visit **Vault Europe's Finance Career Channel** at **www.Vault.com/Europe** for insider firm profiles, employee surveys of banking profesionals in Europe, job listings, expert finance career advice, insider salary information and more.

VAULT   CAREER LIBRARY   127

What is involved on a day-to-day basis? Quite a bit of phone time and quite of bit of dealing with the book.

The book

As mentioned earlier, the "**book**" is a listing of all investors who have indicated interest in buying stock in an offering. Investors place orders by telling their respective salesperson at the investment bank or by calling the syndicate department of the lead manager. Only the lead manager maintains (or carries) the book in a deal.

Orders can come in one of two forms — either an order for a specified number of shares at any price, or for a specified number of shares up to a specified price. Most buy-siders indicate a price range of some kind. Often, large institutions come in with a "10 percent order." That is the goal of the managers, and means that the investor wants to buy 10 percent of the shares in the deal.

In terms of timing, the book comes together during the roadshow, as investors meet the company's management team. Adding to the excitement, many investors wait until the day or two prior to pricing to call in their order. Thus, a manager may not know if they can sell the deal until the very last minute. The day before the securities begin to trade, syndicate looks at the book and calls each potential buyer one last time. It is important to ferret out which money managers are serious about owning the stock/bonds over the long haul. Those that don't are called **flippers**. Why would a money manager choose this strategy? Because in a good market, getting shares in the offering is often a sure way to make money, as stocks usually jump up a few percentage points at the opening bell. However, flippers are the bane of successful offerings. Institutional money managers who buy into public deals just to sell their shares on the first day only cause the stock to immediately trade down.

Pricing and allocation

How does syndicate price a stock? Simple — by supply and demand. There are a fixed number of shares or bonds in a public deal available, and buyers indicate exactly how many shares and at what price they are willing to purchase the securities. The problem is that most deals are **oversubscribed**; i.e., there are more shares demanded than available for sale. Therefore, syndicate must determine how many shares to allocate to each buyer. To add to the headache, because investors know that every successful deal is oversubscribed, they inflate their actual share indications. So, a 10 percent order may in fact mean that the money manager actually wants something like 2 or 3 percent of the deal. The irony, then, is that any money manager that actually got as many shares as she asked for would immediately cancel her order, realizing that the deal was a "dog."

In the end, a combination of syndicate's experience with investors and their instincts about buyers tells them how many shares to give to each buy-sider. Syndicate tries to avoid flippers, but can never entirely do so.

After the book is set, syndicate calls the offering company to report the details. This "**pricing call**," as it is called, occurs immediately after the roadshow ends and the day before the stock begins trading in the market. Pricing calls sometimes results in yelling, cursing and swearing from the management teams of companies going public. Remember that in IPOs, the call is telling founders of companies what their firm is worth — reactions sometimes border on the extreme. If a deal is not hot (as most are not), then the given price may be disappointing to the company. "How can my company not be the greatest thing since sliced bread?" CEOs often think.

Also, company managers often mistakenly believe that the pricing call is some sort of negotiation, and fire back with higher prices. However, only on rare occasions can the CEO influence the final price — and even then only a little. Their negotiating strength stems from the fact that they can walk away from a deal. Managers will then be out months of work and a lot of money (deal expenses can be very high). An untold number of deals have been shelved because the company has insisted on another 50 cents on the offered share price, and the syndicate department has told management that it simply is not feasible. It may sound like a pittance, but on a 20 million share deal, 50 cents per share is a whopping $10 million in proceeds to the company (less underwriting fees).

Politicians

Because of this tension over the offering price, senior syndicate professionals must be able to handle difficult and delicate situations. But it's not just company management that must be handled with care. During a deal, syndicate must also deal with the salesforce, other underwriters, and buy-siders. Similar to the research analyst, the syndicate professional often finds that diplomacy is one of the most critical elements to success. Successful syndicate pros can read between the lines and figure out the real intentions of buy-siders (are they flippers or are they committed to the offering, do they really want 10 percent of the offering, etc.). Also, good syndicate associates are proficient at schmoozing with other investment banks and garnering underwriting business (when the syndicate department is not representing the manager).

Visit **Vault Europe's Finance Career Channel** at **www.Vault.com/Europe** for insider firm profiles, employee surveys of banking profesionals in Europe, job listings, expert finance career advice, insider salary information and more.

VAULT CAREER LIBRARY 129

It's still a bank, not a cocktail party

Although syndicate professionals must have people skills, a knack for number-crunching and market knowledge are also important. Offerings involve many buy orders at various prices and for various levels of stock. Syndicate must allocate down from the biggest institutional investors to the smallest retail client (if retail clients are allowed to get shares in the deal). And pricing is quite a mix of art and science. Judging market momentum, deal interest and company egos can be trying indeed.

Who works in syndicate?

As for the players in syndicate, some have MBAs, and some don't. Some worked their way up, and some were hired directly into an associate syndicate position. The payoffs in syndicate can be excellent for top dogs, however, as the most advanced syndicate pros often deal directly with clients (management teams of companies doing an offering), handle pricing calls, and talk to the biggest investors. They essentially become salespeople themselves, touting the firm, their expertise in placing stock or bonds, and their track record. Occasionally, syndicate MDs will attend an important deal pitch to potential clients, especially if he or she is a good talker. At the same time, some syndicate professionals move into sales or other areas, often in order to get away from the endless politicking involved with working in the syndicate department.

Beginners in the syndicate department help put together the book, schedule roadshow meetings and work their way up to dealing with investors, other I-banks, and internal sales. Because syndicate requires far fewer people than other areas in the bank, fewer job openings are to be found. Rarely does a firm recruit on college campuses for syndicate jobs — instead, firms generally hire from within the industry or from within the firm.

APPENDIX

About the Authors

Richard Roberts is a professor at the University of Sussex, UK. He is author of numerous books and articles on investment banking, the international financial system and international financial centres, especially London.

Tom Lott, born in Dallas, Texas, graduated from Vanderbilt University in 1993. He started in the investment banking business upon graduation, joining Raymond James & Associates, an investment bank in St. Petersburg, Florida. His work experience includes a brief stint in research and four years in corporate finance. He obtained his MBA from the J.L. Kellogg Graduate School of Management (Northwestern), where he served as chairman of the investments club. He now works in fixed income trading at Merrill Lynch in New York City.

Derek Loosvelt is a graduate of the Wharton School at the University of Pennsylvania. He's a Brooklyn-based writer and editor and has worked for Brill's Content and Inside.com. Previously, he worked in investment banking at CIBC and Duff & Phelps.

Visit **Vault Europe's Finance Career Channel** at www.Vault.com/Europe for insider firm profiles, employee surveys of banking profesionals in Europe, job listings, expert finance career advice, insider salary information and more.

V/\ULT   CAREER LIBRARY   **133**

As a responsible publishing company, Vault is proud to work with printers who source materials from well managed sustainable forests: this ensures long term timber supplies and helps protect the environment.

We aim to grow our business while minimizing our impact on the environment.

We encourage readers to download and read the electronic versions of our guides available on our web sites, www.vault.com and www.vault.com/europe.

We are also proud to have installed the Vault Online Career Library at 850 universities worldwide. With the Online Career Library, students worldwide can download electronic versions of our guides as part of their job search preparation. By providing this service to students, Vault and its university partners help reduce the printing and shipping of our guides

By leveraging the latest technology, we aim to contribute responsibly to the world in which we live.

Thomas Nutt
General Manager
Vault Europe